D1272515

How the Automobile Changed the World

Craig E. Blohm

San Diego, CA

About the Author

Craig E. Blohm has written numerous books and magazine articles for young readers. He and his wife, Desiree, reside in Tinley Park, Illinois.

Picture Credits:

Cover: JohnnyH5

4: Richard Thornton/Shutterstock.com (top),
   Uncle Leo/Shutterstock.com (bottom)
5: Roschetzky/Shutterstock.com (top left),
   JasonDoiy/iStockphoto.com (top right),
   jgroup/Thinkstock Images (bottom left),
   Fingerhut/Shutterstock.com (bottom right)
8: Ford car model T in 1908/Tallandier/
   Bridgeman Images
12: Steam-powered car invented by Nicolas
   Joseph Cugnot (1725–1804) in 1771, 1886
   (engraving) (b/w photo), French School, (19th
   century)/Private Collection/Archives Charmet/
   Bridgeman Images
16: Henry Ford (1863–1947) American industrialist
   pioneer of American car industry driving his
   Quadricycle, 1896/PVDE/Bridgeman Images

21: Associated Press
24: VanderWolf Images/Shutterstock.com
28: TierneyMJ/Shutterstock.com
31: Teens at a Drive In (b/w photo)/Underwood
   Archives/UIG/Bridgeman Images
35: Everett Collection/Newscom
40: Alf Ribeiro/Shutterstock.com
43: Associated Press
46: Jens Wolf/dpa/Picture-Alliance/
   Newscom
50: Barteverett/Shutterstock.com
55: Spaghettikku/iStockphoto.com
58: Andrej Sokolow/dpa/Picture-Alliance/
   Newscom
62: Byungsuk Ko/Shutterstock.com
67: chombosan/Shutterstock.com

LIBRARY OF CONGRESS CATALOGING-IN-PUBLICATION DATA

Name: Blohm, Craig E., 1948– author.
Title: How the Automobile Changed the World/by Craig E. Blohm.
Description: San Diego, CA: ReferencePoint Press, Inc., [2018] | Series: How
Science Changed the World | Audience: Grades 9–12. | Includes
bibliographical references and index.
Identifiers: LCCN 2017056350 (print) | LCCN 2017061107 (ebook) | ISBN
9781682824085 (eBook) | ISBN 9781682824078 (hardback)
Subjects: LCSH: Automobiles—History—Juvenile literature. | Technological
innovations—History—Juvenile literature. | United
States—Civilization—20th century—Juvenile literature.
Classification: LCC TL147 (ebook) | LCC TL147 .B5745 2018 (print) | DDC
629.2209—dc23
LC record available at https://lccn.loc.gov/2017056350

CONTENTS

IMPORTANT EVENTS IN THE HISTORY OF AUTOMOBILES

1908
The Model T Ford is produced.

1886
Karl Benz and Gottlieb Daimler invent the first true automobile.

1876
Nikolaus Otto invents the four-cycle internal combustion engine.

1771
Nicolas-Joseph Cugnot invents the first steam-powered vehicle.

1913
Ford introduces the moving assembly line.

| 1760 | / | 1860 | 1890 | 1920 | 1950 |

1947
Car sales boom after the World War II ban on auto production is lifted.

1911
Charles F. Kettering invents the electric starter.

1899
The first automobile fatality is recorded in the United States.

1863
Henry Ford is born in Dearborn, Michigan.

1894
The Electrobat, the first practical electric car, is introduced.

1956
President Dwight D. Eisenhower authorizes the building of the Interstate Highway System.

2009
Google establishes its autonomous car project, which would later be renamed Waymo.

2016
Waymo adds self-driving cars to its fleets in several US cities.

1996
General Motors unveils the EV1 electric car.

1955	1970	1985	2000	2015

1973
Arab nations initiate the first oil embargo against the United States.

2000
The Toyota Prius hybrid is introduced in the United States.

2015
An autonomous car makes a cross-country trip from San Francisco to New York.

1979
The second Arab oil embargo begins.

2006
Elon Musk introduces the Tesla Roadster.

A Revolution in Transportation

There are many years that signify an important milestone in American history: 1776, the year that the colonies declared their independence from England; 1861, which marked the beginning of the bloody Civil War; and 1969, when the first American set foot on the moon. The year 1908 is another such milestone, although few people today recognize its significance. But its importance can hardly be overstated, as 1908 was the year that inventor and industrialist Henry Ford introduced the Model T automobile, a vehicle that revolutionized transportation. "The Model T," writes author Jim Rasenberger, "transformed not only the automotive industry, but, in turn, almost every aspect of how Americans lived and worked."[1] That transformation continues to this day.

Transforming Society

Around the turn of the twentieth century, people either walked, rode horses, or traveled in various types of horse-drawn vehicles to get from one place to another. For long-distance journeys, railroads connected both large cities and small towns. In urban areas, public transportation in the form of trollies and buses carried people to work, stores, and leisure destinations such as theaters and restaurants. But the automobile was making steady inroads into the transportation industry.

In the 1920s—sometimes called the first golden age of the automobile—nearly 26 million cars were sold. The Great Depression of the 1930s and World War II slowed automobile production, but by the 1950s the car was an established part of everyday life—and its impact on society was enormous.

Interstate highways, shopping malls, and fast-food chains are just a few of the things that are a direct result of the automobile's influence. "The American automobile has changed the habits of every member of modern society,"[2] wrote Raymond Loewy, an influential designer of modern appliances, locomotives, and automobiles. The Interstate Highway System allowed people who seldom traveled to take vacations or visit distant relatives. The automobile let city dwellers relocate their families to the suburbs, leaving the dirt, noise, and congestion of the urban environment for a far-flung suburban enclave.

> "The American automobile has changed the habits of every member of modern society."[2]
>
> —Raymond Loewy, industrial designer

The Downside of the Automobile

Of course, the automobile's impact has had negative effects as well. As longtime urban residents fled to the suburbs, the inner cities often suffered from decay, crime, and decreased property values. Instead of living in close-knit city neighborhoods, many suburbanites found their new environments lonely and isolating, and many did not even know their neighbors.

Pollution and traffic jams, as well as deaths and injuries due to accidents, are all part of the price Americans have paid for their love affair with the automobile. As these problems grew with the number of cars on the road, automakers began developing new technologies to combat them. For example, hybrid and electric automobiles now provide a practical alternative to the pollution caused by gasoline-powered cars. To help prevent accidents, power steering and antilock brakes allow drivers to

7

maintain better control of their vehicles. Seat belts and airbags, introduced in the 1950s and 1970s, respectively, keep drivers and passengers safer in crashes. Today's cars have restraints for every occupant and may employ ten or more airbags. One manufacturer, Swedish automaker Volvo, has even installed an exterior airbag on its V40 model to protect pedestrians.

The latest automotive innovations actively sense a dangerous situation. Sensors can detect when a car is driving too close to another vehicle and can alert the driver or automatically slow or stop the car. Warnings are sounded when another vehicle is in the driver's "blind spot" or when the car drifts from its lane. Rear-facing cameras provide a view of objects, such as a bi-

The 1908 Ford Model T was the first mass-produced, affordable automobile. It was easy to operate, rugged and dependable, and relatively simple to maintain and repair.

cycle or a child, not visible to the driver when backing up. Many of today's automobiles can even park themselves, which raises an intriguing question: What is the Future of Driving?

The Future of Driving

Given all the new technological features that make the modern automobile safer and more reliable, one feature may soon become obsolete: the driver. By early 2018 Waymo, a Google company that develops autonomous vehicles, had driven more than 4 million driver-free miles. The true driverless car is still years away; autonomous vehicles are required to have a driver behind the wheel in case of an emergency that the car's software cannot handle.

Over the past century, the automobile has evolved from the primitive Model T to today's almost endless variety of powerful cars. Perhaps more than any other invention, the automobile has changed society, for better and worse. It has given people the opportunity to travel as never before and allowed workers to live far from their jobs. It has transformed the American landscape and permanently altered the American way of life. The automobile, loved by many as a symbol of freedom and tolerated by others as a necessary evil, will continue to be a driving force in society.

CHAPTER 1

Inventing the Horseless Carriage

It is an irony of automotive history that the first self-propelled mechanical vehicle may also have been the first to be involved in an accident. French military engineer Nicolas-Joseph Cugnot had been experimenting with the use of steam power as a way to propel land vehicles for the French army. In 1771 he built what he called a *fardier à vapeur*, or steam cart, for transporting artillery and other military equipment. It was an odd-looking vehicle that employed three wheels, one in front and two in the rear. At the very front was a massive boiler that produced steam to drive pistons that turned the front wheel, moving the vehicle forward.

Cugnot's vehicle had some serious drawbacks. Poor weight distribution made it unable to travel on rough terrain (a necessity for military use), and it had to be stopped every ten to fifteen minutes to relight the boiler. On a test run, so the legend goes, the *fardier*'s driver lost control of the vehicle and it crashed into a brick wall. Despite the failure of his invention on a practical level, Cugnot proved that a mechanically-powered land vehicle—in other words, an automobile—could be built.

Steam and Electricity

Inspired by Cugnot's work, many nineteenth-century inventors experimented with steam-powered vehicles. In

1803 British engineer Richard Trevithick built the London Steam Carriage, a three-wheeled coach that could carry up to eight passengers at about 8 miles per hour (13 kph). In July 1803 the carriage made a 10-mile (16 km) journey through London carrying seven or eight passengers, the world's first trip involving a self-propelled, passenger-carrying vehicle.

Others tried using steam engines to power their own vehicles. Amédée-Ernest Bollée Sr., a French inventor, built several steam-powered vehicles in the 1870s and 1880s. In the United States, J.W. Carhart of Racine, Wisconsin, built a steam automobile in 1873. While driving the car through town, he discovered that the noise so frightened the townspeople that "it was not long before we had all the streets in the town to ourselves, for when they had seen the machine, all the citizens were unanimous in predicting that the thing would blow up."[3]

While steam automobiles were chugging along American roads, another power source for land vehicles was being developed: electricity. The first practical electric car, the Electrobat, was built in 1894 by two Philadelphia engineers. Powered by a battery weighing 1,600 pounds (726 kg), it could travel 50 miles (80 km) between charges. By the turn of the twentieth century, dozens of factories were building and selling electric cars.

With both steam and electric power came drawbacks. Steam cars were noisy and required time to build up enough steam to work, and fear of a boiler explosion, however unlikely, persisted. Electric automobiles were clean and quiet but had limited range, few places to recharge, and batteries that could leak corrosive acid. "All [vehicles] now for sale," commented Joseph Mandery, owner of the Rochester Automobile Company, in 1899, "have too many serious objections to make them commercially practical."[4] But another source of power soon took over and drove the automobile to the peak of global popularity.

The steam-powered vehicle invented by Nicolas-Joseph Cugnot in 1771 looked very different from automobiles today. It had only three wheels, one in front and two in the back.

The Internal Combustion Engine

In 1876 German engineer Nikolaus Otto developed the four-stroke internal combustion engine. Known as the Otto cycle engine, it was powered by a mixture of air and gasoline, which was compressed and ignited by a spark to create an explosion inside a cylinder. That explosion moved a piston, which could be connected to various devices to perform mechanical work such as pumping liquids or running a machine.

Otto's engine was too large to be used in vehicles, but in 1885 one of his employees, Gottlieb Daimler, along with coworker Wilhelm Maybach, developed an engine small enough to propel a motorcycle. The next year Daimler and Maybach invented what many consider the first true automobile, a motor carriage with four wheels powered by a four-stroke gasoline internal combustion engine. Coincidentally, some 60 miles (96.6 km) away in Mannheim, Germany, inventor Karl Benz also unveiled an automobile. Called the Patent-Motorwagen, Benz's vehicle had three wheels, an internal combustion engine, and a bench seat for two.

Daimler and Benz never met, but they share credit for independently inventing the first automobile. At this early stage in automobile history, cars were mostly playthings for the rich. Soon, however, an inventor in Detroit, Michigan, would create a car for the masses.

Henry Ford's New Car

Born on a farm in Dearborn, Michigan, on July 30, 1863, Henry Ford never wanted to follow his father into the farming life. What set young Henry on the path toward building an automobile was an encounter with a steam-powered tractor when he was twelve years old. "I remember that engine as though I had seen it only yesterday, for it was the first vehicle other than horse-drawn that I had ever seen," he wrote, years later. "It was that engine that took me into automotive transportation."[5]

At age seventeen, Ford left home to pursue his dream. His first automobile, which he took for a test drive in Detroit on June 4, 1896, was called the Quadricycle. It was a four-wheeled carriage that accommodated two people and was propelled by a four-horsepower internal combustion gasoline engine. The Quadricycle was not meant to be sold commercially; historian Douglas Brinkley notes that "the only thing that mattered about Henry Ford's Quadricycle was that it worked well enough to keep his mental gears turning toward the development of the modern automobile."[6]

In 1903 Ford officially launched his automobile business, the Ford Motor Company, in Detroit. The company began producing automobiles of ever-increasing power and refinement. It introduced eight different models in its first five years of operation. With a successful company behind him, Ford was ready to transform the automobile industry. "I will build a motor car for the great multitude,"[7] Ford announced. That automobile was the Model T.

> "I will build a motor car for the great multitude."[7]
>
> —Henry Ford, automotive entrepreneur

On October 1, 1908, the first Model T rolled out of Ford's manufacturing plant on Piquette Avenue in Detroit. Powered by a twenty-horsepower gasoline engine, the car, affectionately known as the Tin Lizzie, could attain a speed of 45 miles per hour (72.4 kph). It was available in several body styles, from a two-seat runabout to a town car that could accommodate seven people. The initial price for a five-seat Model T was $850, not including useful options such as a top, a windshield, bumpers, or headlights. The Model T was an immediate success. People who had never driven a car before now flocked to Ford dealers. But the Model T was not just for driving. With the car jacked up, the rear wheels could be used to run equipment such as power saws for lumber yards. Therefore, farmers often converted their Model Ts into tractors and threshers.

The first Models Ts were assembled one at a time in the Piquette Avenue factory in what was essentially a stationary assembly line. The chassis, or frame, of each car remained at a particular spot on the factory floor. Workers called runners brought parts for the cars from storage areas to the chassis, where skilled craftspeople assembled the automobile by hand. Only when the car was finished would it roll out of the factory, with another bare chassis replacing it. This method of handcrafting automobiles required numerous skilled and unskilled workers and was time consuming: It took 12.5 hours to build one Model T. With orders piling up, Ford needed a new production method to keep up with the demand. He developed what would change forever the way products were manufactured: the moving assembly line.

Inventing the Modern Age

When Ford moved his manufacturing operation into a new factory in Highland Park, Michigan, in 1910, he was already considering ways to speed up production of the Model T. While Ford is often credited with inventing the assembly line, it really dates back to ancient civilizations, such as the Egyptian and Assyrian. In truth, Ford took other inventors' ideas about modern mass production and improved on their methods—but it was his improvements

How an Internal Combustion Engine Works

The modern internal combustion engine is a marvel of engineering not much different from the engines that Nikolaus Otto developed in 1876. The internal combustion engine incorporates four, six, or more pistons, each traveling up and down within a closed cylinder inside the engine. The up-and-down movement of the pistons is transformed into rotary motion via a crankshaft, which ultimately provides motive power to the vehicle's wheels.

Internal combustion engines create power in a series of four cycles, or strokes. In the first, or intake, stroke, the piston moves to the bottom of the cylinder, drawing in a mixture of gasoline and air through a valve in the top. During the next stroke, compression, the piston moves up, squeezing the fuel-air mixture to increase its combustibility. In the third, or combustion, stroke, a spark plug at the top of the cylinder fires, causing the fuel-air mixture to explode and drive the piston downward. This creates the energy to turn the crankshaft. The final stroke, the exhaust stroke, causes the piston to move upward once more, pushing the gases from the explosion out of the cylinder through another valve.

Internal combustion engines that run on diesel fuel rather than gasoline do not have spark plugs. The heat created by the compression of the diesel-air mixture in the cylinder is enough to ignite it without the need for a spark.

---

that made all the difference. Ford decided to introduce a moving assembly line.

"The first step in assembly," Ford recalled in his autobiography, "came when we began taking the work to the men instead of the men to the work."[8] Inspiration for the moving assembly-line idea came in a peculiar way. In 1912 several Ford employees (some accounts say it was Ford himself) took a tour of a Chicago meatpacking plant. The men marveled at the well-organized operation. Animal carcasses moved by an overhead conveyor to various workstations, where workers carved cuts of meat before the carcass progressed to the next station. The process was extremely efficient, so the Ford men wondered whether it would work in a different environment, such as an automobile factory. One man who had no doubt was Ford foreman William Klann, who later recalled, "I went down to Chicago to the slaughterhouse myself. I came back and said, 'If they can kill pigs and cows that way, we can build cars and build motors that way.'" Klann's supervisor was skeptical, but said, "Well, see what you can do."[9]

This new concept was first tested on the assembly of the fly-wheel magneto, a part that produced the spark that ignited the air and gasoline mixture in the Model T's engine. Instead of one man building a complete magneto, the job was divided into separate steps. One worker performed his specific task, and then the magneto moved by conveyor belt to the next worker, who performed his function. This method reduced the time it took to build one magneto from twenty minutes to just over thirteen minutes. Soon, other subassemblies such as dashboards, radia-

Industrialist Henry Ford sits on his Quadricycle in 1896. This experimental vehicle was never meant to be mass-produced. Instead, it proved to Ford that gasoline-powered vehicles could be manufactured from common resources.

tors, and complete engines were being built in a similar manner, and Ford decided that the entire car should be built in the same way, as he noted in his autobiography. "One man is now able to do [the work that] more than four did only a comparatively few years ago. That [magneto] line established the efficiency of the method and we now use it everywhere. The assembling of the motor, formerly done by one man, is now divided into eighty-four operations—those men do the work that three times their number formerly did."[10]

The initial moving assembly line consisted of a Model T chassis being pulled by a rope and windlass system across the factory floor. As the chassis progressed along the 150-foot (45.7 m) line, each worker stood at his assigned position and performed one specific task before the chassis moved on. One worker, for example, might insert a bolt into a hole, another might put on the nut, and a third would tighten it. When the next chassis reached the worker's station, he repeated his task, and so on throughout his nine-hour shift. In 1914 the rope system was replaced by an electrically powered endless chain drive that pulled the cars along the assembly line. Soon, notes auto journalist Tony Swan, the Highland Park plant "was a maze of conveyors, powered drive belts, overhead traveling cranes, and hundreds of machine tools. Moving assembly went into full swing."[11]

Improving the Assembly Line

As with any new technology, there were problems to be solved and improvements to be made. Factory supervisors experimented with alternately speeding up and slowing down the line in order to determine the ideal speed for the most productivity. Early on, some workers who were assembling crankcases suffered broken legs when the 120-pound (54.4 kg) part fell on them from the assembly line. Better clamps to secure the crankcases to the conveyor belt solved the problem. Many men complained of sore backs due to the constant bending required to perform their assigned task, a problem alleviated by raising conveyors so that workers no longer had to stoop. Then there was the monotony of performing the same task over and over again. It was a mind-numbing job that resulted in many employees quitting after just a few days on the line. Ford enticed his workers to stay by raising their wages to an unheard-of five dollars a day, more than twice the average rate. Work shifts went from nine hours to eight, and a five-day work-week was instituted.

The assembly line "had a huge, huge impact," says Northwestern University professor Stephen Burnett. "Any time you increase the productivity of labor, tremendously valuable things can happen to the economy."[12] The moving assembly line was so efficient that the time it took to build one Model T fell from 12 hours to just 1.5 hours. In addition, as production increased, the car's price fell dramatically. By 1924 a Model T touring car, which initially sold for $850, could be bought for $290. Finally, just about everyone could afford his or her own personal transportation. By the time the Model T was discontinued in 1927, Ford had sold more than 15 million of the sturdy little Tin Lizzies.

> "Any time you increase the productivity of labor, tremendously valuable things can happen to the economy."[12]
>
> —Stephen Burnett, professor, Northwestern University

From Line Workers to Co-bots

The same year that production of the Model T ended, Ford replaced it with the Model A, which was just as successful as its predecessor. Rather than keeping his production methods for his own use, Ford eagerly shared the advantages of the moving assembly line with other automobile manufacturers. General Motors, or GM, (founded in 1908) and Chrysler (founded in 1925) had joined Ford in what would become known as the Big Three auto companies and soon incorporated the system in their factories.

Ford's Social Experiment

One of the biggest problems facing Henry Ford and his moving assembly line was worker turnover. According to the Henry Ford Heritage Association, Ford had to hire four men for every job at his Highland Park plant just to make up for those who failed to show up for their shifts. Ford's five-dollar-an-hour wage solved the problem but came with conditions.

In March 1913 Ford established the Sociological Department to provide employees with an array of benefits such as medical care and low-cost home loans. When the five-dollar wage was instituted the next year, Ford created guidelines that workers were required to follow to qualify for the raise. The Sociological Department sent investigators unannounced to employees' homes to evaluate their living conditions and spending habits and determine whether their children were attending school. Consequences for workers who failed to live up to the strict standards included having their pay reduced, being denied advancement, and possibly losing their job.

Ford's program succeeded in reducing the turnover rate to just 16 percent by 1915, compared to 370 percent two years before. But regulating employee behavior eventually proved too controversial to continue. Even Ford himself changed his mind, writing, "Paternalism has no place in industry. Welfare work that consists in prying into employees' private concerns is out of date." The Sociology Department became inactive in 1921 and was officially closed in 1948.

Henry Ford, *My Life and Work*. New York: Classic House, 2009, p. 98.

Throughout the 1930s the automobile had made profound changes in industry and society. During World War II the moving assembly line enabled the United States to become the "arsenal of democracy," with auto plants building tanks, trucks, and airplanes in overwhelming numbers for the war effort. Eventually, not only automakers but companies making everything from appliances to frozen foods took advantage of the efficiency of the moving assembly line.

In the twenty-first century, assembly lines look vastly different from Ford's groundbreaking factory in Highland Park. Robots are now commonplace on the factory floor, welding joints, moving raw materials, and assembling products. They can perform these tasks with greater precision than humans without needing a coffee break or a day off. But that does not mean human workers are headed for extinction. In its German plant, Ford is experimenting with "co-bots," robots that work side by side with humans on the assembly line to insure that the best quality is maintained. "If we deem that is efficient enough," Ford public relations manager Karl Henkel says, "we can take a look at including them in other plants. The co-bots are an 'and' proposition and not an 'or' proposition. It's not 'can this robot do what a worker cannot do?' They're complementary, working together as a team."[13]

Electric car manufacturer Tesla builds its vehicles in a 5-million-square-foot (464,515 sq m) state-of-the-art factory in Fremont, California. Henry Ford would scarcely recognize Tesla's version of his assembly line, where 160 high-tech robots and six thousand workers can produce two thousand electric cars every week. Tesla vice president Gilbert Passin explains how the company has adapted modern assembly-line technology. "We have these super-elegant robots we call smart carts, where every car is essentially moving through the factory by itself. It follows a magnetic strip and, essentially, the car is being assembled from the inside out. We are utilizing automation to the fullest. We have a variety of robots from teeny little ones to huge ones that are able to move the entire [automobile] body itself."[14]

> "We have a variety of robots from teeny little ones to huge ones that are able to move the entire [automobile] body itself."[14]
>
> —Gilbert Passin, vice president, Tesla Motors

Ford has also taken its own assembly-line technology into the twenty-first century with its virtual manufacturing process. Using motion-capture technology developed in the feature film industry, Ford engineers digitize the body movements of workers simulating the tasks they would perform on the assembly line. These move-

Robots at the Tesla plant in Fremont, California, carry on the ideal set by Henry Ford: the rapid manufacture of automobiles along an assembly line.

ments are then analyzed to determine the best way to design the assembly-line operation to minimize the strain and injuries that workers may suffer during the manufacturing process. The use of virtual reality goggles and 3D-printed mock-ups of various auto components help Ford engineers create a virtual situation that closely simulates a worker's actions on the real assembly line.

Whether making a microwave oven, a cell phone, or a new car, Henry Ford's moving assembly line changed the world of manufacturing and made life easier and more productive for people all over the world. Once, later in his life, Ford's opinions on a particular subject were challenged by a student. "These are different times: This is the modern age," the student scolded the old inventor. "Young man," Ford replied, "I invented the modern age."[15] Even today, few would disagree.

CHAPTER 2

The Indispensable Automobile

Americans who wanted to buy a car during World War II were simply out of luck. Between February 1942 and October 1945, automobile manufacturers halted the production of new consumer cars and trucks so their assembly lines could turn out matériel for the war effort. By the fall of 1944, the war was entering its final stages, and automakers began looking forward to resuming the production of automobiles. People had been saving money during the war, and cars were among the first things on their wish lists. When World War II ended, the American public's pent-up desire for new automobiles exploded.

The Modern Automobile

In 1945 automobile manufacturers began producing cars for the 1946 model year. Government restrictions on developing new automobile designs during the war meant the new cars were actually prewar designs slightly changed for the postwar market. "The 1946 and '47 Chevys were just '42s with new grilles and trim,"[16] recalls vintage auto restorer Stephen Kassiss. But the car-buying public was not deterred: In 1946 sales rocketed to over 2 million passenger cars and in 1947 to more than 3.5 million. Most of these cars were produced by the Big Three, but several independent automakers also prospered. In 1947 one of these companies came up with the first new automobile design of the postwar period.

The Studebaker Company had entered the automobile business in 1902 and was a manufacturer of reliable cars until the World War II freeze. In 1947 Studebaker's advertising boasted "First by Far with a Post-War Car" when it rolled out its sleek new Starlight coupe. The Starlight had a radical new look that featured a trunk almost as long as the hood and a unique wraparound rear window that gave backseat passengers a panoramic view of the passing scenery. By comparison, the Fords, Chevrolets, and Dodges with their bulky prewar designs suddenly seemed old-fashioned and boring.

It did not take long for the Big Three to gear up their production of up-to-date designs to attract new customers. By the 1950s the auto manufacturers were competing to see which one could outdo the others in adding chrome, tail fins, and luxury features to their vehicles.

The Automobile Decade

The competition actually began in 1948, when GM designers added small fins to the company's new Cadillac, its top-of-the-line brand. Before long, American automobiles were sporting tail fins that grew larger during the 1950s. "The heads of the [Big Three] design teams," notes Automotive Hall of Fame president Jeff Leestma, "clearly tried to out-do each other, year after year, to see who could wow the public with the next, biggest, sharpest tail fin."[17] The high point of tail fin architecture, both literally and figuratively, was reached in the design of the 1959 Cadillac. With soaring, winglike fins punctuated by bullet-shaped taillights, the car looked like a jet plane ready to take off. In fact, the first tail fins "were a response to America's post-war fascination with the jet age,"[18] says Leestma.

Chrome was also a defining factor in 1950s automotive design. From massive front bumpers to body trim and rear taillight surrounds, chrome gleamed in the auto showrooms to entice prospective buyers. Another important feature was the use of color. Gone were the days when Henry Ford reportedly said of his Model T, "Any customer can have a car painted any color

In the 1950s, car companies competed by adding luxury interiors and stylistic exteriors. This 1959 Cadillac, for example, showcases a large body, bullet tail lights, rear fins, and whitewall tires.

that he wants, so long as it is black."[19] Midcentury cars sported newly popular pastels of pink and green, and two-tone paint schemes could be ordered. As cars grew more elaborately decorated, they also grew longer, lower, and wider. According to Harley Earl, design chief for three decades at GM, "My primary purpose for twenty-eight years has been to lengthen and lower the American automobile, at times in reality and always at least in appearance."[20]

> "My primary purpose for twenty-eight years has been to lengthen and lower the American automobile."[20]
>
> —Harley Earl, design chief, GM

Although automakers were selling lots of cars, they were always looking for ways to increase sales. One consequence of this was a rather dubious strategy called planned obsolescence. In order to make owners dissatisfied with their current automobile, manufacturers began changing the looks of their vehicles every year. New cars might sport more chrome or a sleeker profile than the previous year's models. John DeLorean, a former GM executive, noted, "Year in and year out, we were urging Americans to sell their cars and buy new ones because the styling had changed. There was really no reason for them to change from one model to the next, except for new wrinkles in the sheet metal."[21] Although planned obsolescence succeeded in selling more cars, it also caused people to replace rather than repair a perfectly good car, whether they could afford it or not. The constant turnover of vehicles also had an environmental impact, leaving more automobiles rusting away in junkyards or overloading landfills.

The Need for Speed

While planned obsolescence had automobile designers tinkering with a car's outward appearance, engineers were doing their own tinkering under the hood. As cars got larger and heavier, engines also needed to evolve in order to adequately power the vehicles. Most mid-century cars had a variety of engines from which customers could choose. The 1957 Chevrolet, one of the most iconic cars of the 1950s, offered eight different engines, from a 140-horsepower 6-cylinder to a 283-horsepower 8-cylinder. Other manufacturers also offered numerous engines and gave them exciting nicknames, such as Skyrocket, Power Flow, and Strato-Streak. The muscle car, a lightweight, sporty auto powered by a high-performance engine, became a favorite of 1960s hot-rodders, who did not shy away from an occasional street race. Bigger engines and more horsepower meant more gasoline consumed. The large, fuel-hungry cars of the era were often referred to as gas guzzlers, but for the most part, fuel consumption was not an issue. Gas was cheap, with 1 gallon (3.8 L) costing twenty-seven cents in 1950, rising to only thirty-one cents by the end of the decade.

> "Year in and year out, we were urging Americans to sell their cars and buy new ones because the styling had changed."[21]
>
> —John DeLorean, former GM executive

The automobile decade in America saw enormous increases in car ownership. The year 1955 was a banner year for the industry, with 7,466,000 automobiles sold. By 1958 more than 67 million cars were registered, more than twice as many as at the beginning of the decade.

The Dark Side of the Automobile

Two serious automobile-related problems accompanied the meteoric rise in car ownership: accidents and impaired driving. The first US auto fatality, an unlucky man named Henry Bliss, occurred in New York City in 1899. By the early 1970s, auto accidents were causing more than fifty thousand fatalities annually. Numerous factors in collisions include distracted driving, alcohol or drug use, excessive speed, the inexperience of young drivers, and physical impairment of elderly motorists. Automobile manufacturers responded by equipping cars with safety improvements, from seat belts in the 1950s and airbags in the 1970s to antilock brakes in the 1970s and traction control in the 1980s that give drivers better control of their vehicles.

The first recorded drunk driving accident occurred in England in 1897. In 1910 New York became the first state to pass a drunk driving law. California was next, and soon all states had similar laws on the books. The legal limit for a person to be considered drunk—as measured by the amount of alcohol in the blood (blood alcohol concentration, or BAC)—was a BAC of .15 percent in the 1930s. Through the years the BAC was lowered, first to .10 percent and then to the current .08.

By the 1970s drunk driving was a factor in more than 60 percent of highway fatalities. Most affected were the young, with two-thirds of traffic deaths of persons aged sixteen to twenty involving alcohol impairment. Since then, drunk driving fatalities have gone down, thanks to stricter law enforcement, prevention programs, and education about the risks of drinking and driving. But even today the numbers are alarming. Every day in America, twenty-eight people die in alcohol-related traffic accidents—more

Unsafe at Any Speed?

By the late 1950s Americans were becoming tired of the excesses of Detroit's gas guzzlers; they wanted something different. The automotive industry reacted by building smaller, more economical compact cars. GM's entry into the compact car market was unlike any other American automobile.

The Chevrolet Corvair differed in many ways from the typical Detroit automobile. Its engine, made of lightweight aluminum, was located in the rear of the car. It was cooled by air, rather than water as in standard engines. Although a compact car, the Corvair was roomy enough to accommodate six passengers. In producing such a radically different car, GM took a big gamble—one it was destined to lose.

Placing the Corvair's engine directly over the rear driving wheels was meant to provide better stability, but it also gave the front wheels that steered the car poor traction. Reports of crashes flooded GM's headquarters, and soon a young attorney named Ralph Nader began questioning the Corvair's basic design. In a book titled *Unsafe at Any Speed*, Nader accused GM of knowing about the handling problem but ignoring it. The book became a best seller, while sales of the Corvair plummeted.

A subsequent study concluded that the Corvair was no more dangerous to drive than any other car. But the damage was done, and GM discontinued the car in 1969. The Corvair's legacy did contain one bright spot: It made it easier for consumers to bring product-liability lawsuits against negligent manufacturers.

than ten thousand lives lost each year. Although neither the automobile nor alcohol will ever disappear from society, work remains to keep them a safe distance from each other.

The Interstate Highway System

With the increasing number of cars on the roads in the mid-twentieth century, the old infrastructure that had served the nation in the Model T era was proving to be woefully inadequate. Americans needed new highways, and in Washington, DC, they had a president who agreed.

President Dwight D. Eisenhower had learned a lot about roads in his military career. As an army lieutenant in 1919, he joined a convoy that traveled 3,000 miles (4,828 km) across the United States to evaluate the suitability of US highways to transport troops and weapons in the event of an attack. In World War II, as the general in charge of the D-Day invasion, he became familiar with Germany's high-speed superhighway system, the *Reichsautobahn*.

As president, Eisenhower had the authority to create a US road system similar to the *Reichsautobahn*. The German highways were four-lane thoroughfares (two lanes in each direction) that featured a central median and allowed limited access from other roads to eliminate congestion. Eisenhower saw the advantages this system could offer America. As he wrote in his 1963 memoir, "More than any single action by the government since the end of the war, this one would change the face of America with straightaways, cloverleaf turns, bridges, and elongated parkways. Its impact on the American economy—the jobs it would produce in manufacturing and construction, the rural areas it would open up—was beyond calculation."[22]

When President Eisenhower backed highway-building legislation in the 1950s, he probably never envisioned modern-day traffic. Instead, he hoped highways would aid interstate transportation, increase tourism, and open up rural America.

On June 29, 1956, Eisenhower signed the Federal-Aid Highway Act into law. The new law authorized the spending of $25 billion over ten years to create a 41,000-mile (65,983 km) network of highways spanning the United States. Construction began within months, but despite the ten-year deadline, it was not completed until 1992. The current Interstate Highway System comprises 46,876 miles (75,440 km) of paved, limited-access highways stretching from Boston to Seattle and from the Canadian border to the Florida Keys.

The thousands of miles of interstate highways, and the automobiles that motivated their creation, have had an almost immeasurable impact on America. While many of those impacts were indeed beneficial, others created unforeseen problems.

A Changing Landscape

The ribbons of concrete that spread out over the American countryside had an impact that was a combination of good and bad. Most affected by the construction of the interstates were American farmers. The majority of the new roads were in rural areas. Nearly 1 million acres (404,686 ha) of land were acquired by the government, which impacted all or part of about seventy-five thousand farms. The new highways often caused drainage problems and affected soil conservation efforts. With fewer local roads connecting to the interstates, farmers had to drive several miles out of their way to access the new highways. But there were advantages, too. Farmers living near the completed interstates who wished to sell their land were able to get three to four times its agricultural value. The interstates also provided a quicker way to get produce to urban markets, and part-time farmers could travel to their nonfarm jobs faster.

As farming was changing, so the housing industry was booming with postwar construction. The automobile allowed city workers to relocate from crowded urban areas to the fresh air and open spaces of the suburbs. One of the earliest postwar suburbs was Levittown, a sprawling planned community of single-family homes built by William Levitt in Nassau County, New York. Begun

The Mother Road

Before the vast network of highways known as the Interstate Highway System was created, there was one single road on which Americans could travel all the way from the Midwest to the West Coast. It had many names, including the Will Rogers Highway and Main Street of America. But it is best remembered by its official designation: Route 66.

Begun in 1926, Route 66 eventually connected Chicago with Los Angeles, a distance of 2,448 miles (3,940 km), meandering through eight states in the Midwest and Southwest. When the Dust Bowl, a devastating period of severe drought and dust storms, hit the American prairie in the 1930s, desperate farmers loaded their cars with all their possessions and took Route 66 to California in search of work. The plight of these migrants was portrayed in the novel *The Grapes of Wrath* by John Steinbeck, who dubbed Route 66 "the mother road." The road's fame peaked in the 1960s with a TV show and a catchy song that invited Americans to "get your kicks on Route 66."

When the Interstate Highway System became the preferred mode of travel for American motorists, traffic on Route 66 sharply declined, and in 1985 it was decommissioned as an official US highway. But the iconic route's popularity never died out. Several Route 66 associations have been established to keep the memory of the mother road alive, and even today nostalgic motorists can still get their kicks on many remaining stretches of Route 66.

John Steinbeck, *The Grapes of Wrath.* New York: Viking, 2014, p. 123.

Quoted in Route-66.com, "Get Your Kicks on Route 66: The Song Linked to the Road." www.theroute-66.com/get-your-kicks.html.

in 1947 to accommodate the flood of men returning from the war, Levittown was just a 25-mile (40.2 km) commute from New York City. Taking a cue from the auto industry, Levitt mass-produced his houses; workers performed a single task and then moved on to work on the next house. He also adopted the planned obsolescence of the automakers, changing each year's house designs to attract buyers. By the time Levittown was completed in 1951, it had 17,447 homes. Levitt had created the American Dream of home ownership and was called the father of the suburb.

Suburban women were often the beneficiaries of the automobile, which freed them from being stuck at home while their husbands were at work. Daily walks to a local grocer were replaced by weekly trips to a supermarket, where a variety of food awaited the homemaker. For suburban teenagers, getting a driver's license was a highly anticipated rite of passage. They, too, were liberated from being homebound, with a growing number of drive-in theaters, fast-food restaurants, and other hangouts beckoning them.

But despite the advantages of freedom, good schools, and low crime rates, life in the suburbs was not perfect. Many suburbanites felt isolated, cocooned in individual houses separated by lawns and shrubbery. Many suburbanites barely knew their neighbors, with a wave and a nod replacing conversations held on an urban apartment house's stoop.

Life in 1960s suburbia was also increasingly sedentary. The automobile replaced walking as the main form of transportation, and there were few places that could be reached without piling

American lifestyles changed in the 1950s because of automobile ownership. More teenagers, for example, had access to vehicles and looked forward to getting a driver's license.

into the family car. Still, the problems experienced by suburban-ites were minor compared to those left behind in the cities.

The Automobile in the Cities

As the automobile drove more people to the suburbs, urban ar-eas suffered from the effect of this migration. Population declines triggered the deterioration of many cities—including, ironically, De-troit, the birthplace of the American automobile. Government was spending more money building roads, so there was less funding for urban mass transit, which was essential for people who could not afford cars.

When the path of the interstates encountered urban areas, they were usually routed through the poorest sections of the cit-ies, where property was cheap. From New York to Los Angeles, urban minority neighborhoods were destroyed or altered beyond recognition. Residents who were not displaced had to live with the noise and pollution of thousands of cars zooming through their neighborhoods. In 1968 a handbook published by the Fed-eral Highway Administration tried to put a positive spin on urban highways, noting, "Some internal freeways have been deliberately located through the worst slums to help the city in its program of slum clearance and urban renewal."[23]

If the freeways divided the urban poor from the suburban middle class, automobile ownership itself became a mark of so-cial status. As authors Catherine Lutz and Anne Lutz Fernandez remark in their book, *Carjacked*, "In a world where transporta-tion is centered on a road built for cars, you must be a driver to achieve the valued status of a truly independent person. Unli-censed and carless adults know this better than most; they cope with the anxiety or guilt of relying on others for rides or the shame of seeming somehow immature, inadequate, or incompetent."[24]

Gas guzzlers, muscle cars, and the family sedan are all part of the long history of the US auto industry. Americans have embraced the automobile in all its forms and have created a bond between human and machine that will be difficult, if not impossible, to break.

CHAPTER 3

Crisis at the Pump

America is a nation of automobiles and drivers. Americans pride themselves on being self-reliant, and the automobile has become a large part of that mind-set. Sometimes, however, that self-reliance can be shattered by unanticipated circumstances.

On October 6, 1973, troops and tanks of the Egyptian and Syrian armies staged a surprise attack against Israel in retribution for Israel's victory in a war against Egypt, Syria, and Jordan six years earlier. Alarmed by the sudden assault on America's ally, President Richard M. Nixon authorized sending military equipment to Israel. Although this helped the Israelis gain the upper hand in the war, there would be consequences. According to the *New York Times*, the administration was "deeply concerned about the repercussions it could have on relations with oil-producing Arab states."[25] It did not take long for those repercussions to occur.

The Arab Oil Embargo

In retaliation for the US support of Israel, Arab members of the Organization of the Petroleum Exporting Countries (OPEC)—a group that included the oil-rich nations of Iran, Iraq, and Saudi Arabia—raised prices on the crude oil they produced, from three dollars to five dollars a barrel (it would jump to twelve dollars in 1974). In a further act of revenge, OPEC imposed an embargo on October 19, shutting off the oil supply line to the United States.

Many Americans were shocked to learn of the embargo, unaware that some of America's oil came from the Middle East. To keep up with growing consumer demand, in 1973 the United States was importing about 35 percent of the oil it used. That oil was critical for a nation that, according to historian Thomas Borstelmann, "used vastly more oil than any other nation, thanks to a fourfold increase since 1945 in the number of cars and trucks on the country's extensive highway network."[26]

> "We are heading toward the most acute shortages of energy since World War II."[27]
>
> —President Richard M. Nixon

Foreign oil not only helps keep cars on the road, it powers factories, produces electricity, heats homes, and is essential for producing plastic for millions of products ranging from ballpoint pens to fertilizer. When that source was cut off by the embargo, Americans began to feel the effects. In a televised address on November 7, Nixon announced the energy emergency.

Most of the Middle Eastern oil producers have reduced overall production and cut off their shipments of oil to the United States. By the end of this month, more than 2 million barrels a day of oil we expected to import into the United States will no longer be available. We must, therefore, face up to a very stark fact: We are heading toward the most acute shortages of energy since World War II. . . . The immediate shortage will affect the lives of each and every one of us. In our factories, our cars, our homes, our offices, we will have to use less fuel than we are accustomed to using.[27]

Nixon urged Americans to lower their thermostats to save on home heating fuel. He proposed that Congress temporarily relax

In 1973 several Middle Eastern governments instituted an embargo on oil to the United States. Throughout that year and the next, car owners sat in long lines at gas stations and paid high prices for fuel.

environmental regulations to balance the nation's fuel consumption and restrict working hours for businesses. The oil embargo affected all areas of American life, but the most visible hardships came on the roads and at the gas stations.

A Disaster for Drivers

In February 1974 Peggy Galgano, a nursing student in New York, had to fill up her gas tank to get to her college classes. Her search for a gas station that still had fuel took most of her day. "They closed down four lines on me this morning,"[28] Galgano lamented. After finally getting into a gas station line that afternoon, she was dismayed to see fifty cars ahead of her. Stories like Galgano's were playing out all across the country as the effects of the embargo deepened in late 1973 and early 1974.

People rose early to try to beat others to the gas pumps. Some stations displayed color-coded signs: Green meant gas was available and red that their supply had run out. Many stations limited

Another Energy Crisis

Just a few years after the Arab oil embargo of 1973, the United States was hit with another energy crisis. Once again, events in the Middle East triggered a gasoline shortage in America. In 1979 the shah of Iran, who was friendly to the United States, was overthrown and replaced by an Islamic republic under the leadership of Ayatollah Ruhollah Khomeini. The political turmoil in Iran had an effect on the country's oil production.

The ayatollah reduced Iran's crude oil output to 4.8 million barrels a day, about 7 percent of the world's oil supply. As in 1973, this reduction in oil production had an effect on the United States. Drivers once again lined up around the block trying to get at least a few gallons of gas before the station's supply was gone. Signs saying "Sorry, No Gas" were again a familiar sight at gas stations, and the sounds of blaring horns filled the air as motorists grew impatient with the long delays.

President Jimmy Carter called the crisis "a clear and present danger to our nation." He urged Americans to lower their thermostats to save energy and devised a plan to ration gas similar to the quotas imposed during World War II. The government even printed ration coupons, but the plan was never executed. The 1979 oil crisis reminded Americans of the nation's continued dependence on foreign oil, as well as the automobile's part in continuing that dependence.

Jimmy Carter, "Energy and the National Goals—a Crisis of Confidence," American Rhetoric. www.americanrhetoric.com.

fill-ups to 10 gallons (38 L) or less, forcing drivers to go from station to station to fill their tanks. Car owners bought locking gas caps to prevent thieves from siphoning off their valuable fuel. Long lines of cars winding around the streets near gas stations (and, ironically, wasting gas by idling) became a familiar sight in American cities. Not surprisingly, tempers often flared, sometimes culminating in fistfights between frustrated drivers jockeying for position in the gas lines. One angry driver reportedly told a gas station attendant, "You are going to give me gas or I will kill you."[29]

While coping with the Arab oil embargo was costly and exasperating for the average driver, for those who made their living driving, it was a matter of economic survival. "We're in this for the money," noted long-haul truck driver Russ Cramer. "We've got forty to fifty thousand dollars tied up in these machines. You can't make money now; you end up working for nothing."[30] Independent truckers like Cramer, who owned their own rigs and relied on a sufficient supply of diesel fuel to do their jobs, blamed the government for not doing enough to alleviate the oil crisis.

"Nobody realizes how important we are to this country," exclaimed one exasperated trucker. "You shut down the trucks, and the country shuts down in 24 hours."[31] To make their frustration clear, the truckers began to protest. On December 4, 1973, a big rig blockade halted traffic on Interstate 80 in Pennsylvania. In New Jersey eighteen hundred truckers caused a seven-hour backup along Interstate 95; similar obstructions tied up numerous interstates from Indiana to Tennessee. The truckers promised to protest until the Nixon administration took steps to lower the price of fuel and ease fill-up restrictions.

> "You shut down the trucks, and the country shuts down in 24 hours."[31]
>
> —Long-haul truck driver

In February 1974 the truckers made good on their threat to go on strike. "We've definitely been mistreated by Washington," declared trucker J.W. Edwards. "I think we are a long way from ending this mess."[32] The strike spread to numerous states, mostly in the eastern United States, and often resulted in violence—including shootings, beatings, and vandalism—against nonstriking truckers. Several governors called out the National Guard to help curb the violence, and workers in many industries had to be laid off due to the lack of materials that were ordinarily delivered to them by truck.

The strike lasted eleven days. In the end, the truckers went back to work after the government promised to impose a surcharge on freight to help defray the higher cost of diesel fuel and guaranteed to make more fuel available to the trucking industry.

Congress stepped up the federal response to the oil crisis by enacting the National Maximum Speed Law. Based on studies that sought to determine the most fuel-efficient speed, the law set 55 miles per hour (88.5 kph) as the top legal speed across the nation. In signing the new law, Nixon said, "Estimates indicate that we can save nearly 200,000 barrels of fuel a day by observing a national limit of 55 miles an hour."[33] Some states had already lowered their speed limit to 55 miles per hour or lower; states with higher limits would have to comply with the law to continue receiving federal funds. Most drivers, however, routinely ignored the law. The anticipated fuel savings of the new speed limit were later determined to be minimal: Gasoline consumption fell by only .02 percent to 1.0 percent. Long after the oil embargo ended, the law remained on the books due to evidence that seemed to suggest lower speeds did result in fewer accidents. Subsequent studies could not confirm this, however, and the law was eventually repealed.

Facing a New Reality

One thing that US automakers had learned by the 1970s was that big cars meant big profits. Building a 1973 Cadillac, for example, cost GM only $300 more than building a Chevrolet, but the luxury car sold for $2,700 more than the Chevy, bringing in a handsome $2,400 in extra profit. Many Americans were willing to pay top dollar for the prestige of owning a large, gas-guzzling car—that is, until the oil crisis hit. With the price of gasoline jumping from thirty cents per gallon in 1958 to sixty-three cents in 1978, cars that got only around 10 miles per gallon (4.25 km/L) suddenly seemed needlessly wasteful and expensive to drive. As car buyers began looking for smaller, more economical vehicles, US auto manufacturers began producing compact cars to meet the demand. In doing so, however, the Big Three created cars that were cheaply made, unreliable, and often ridiculed for poor styling. To find more reliable, fuel-efficient transportation, Americans began turning to cars made by Japanese companies like Toyota, Honda, and Nissan.

With no domestic oil production of its own, Japan has always relied on foreign oil to survive. For the Japanese automotive sector, that meant building cars that were small and energy efficient—the exact opposite of most American automobiles. "When the automotive world was dominated by V-8 Chevrolets and three-ton Cadillacs," notes automotive journalist Peter Cheney, "it was hard to believe that you could make a car that was both light and tough."[34] But that was just the kind of car that Japanese automakers were building.

America began importing Japanese cars in the 1950s, but these early models were generally poorly built and considered unattractive compared to US autos. By the 1970s, however, Japanese cars had improved in quality and gained a reputation for reliability and fuel economy. Many Americans quickly decided to spend their money on Japanese imports. In 1975 Honda sold more than 102,000 Civics in the United States, compared to 38,357 two years earlier, and US automakers were beginning to feel the pinch. In 1973 Chevrolet had built more than 2.5 million vehicles. In 1975 only 823,000 rolled off the assembly line. Ford and Chrysler suffered similar declines in production. In 1982 Honda became the first Japanese automaker to open a factory in the United States to build cars for the US market. Nissan followed in 1983, as did Mazda in 1987. With consumer interest in foreign cars growing, the 1980s saw the Big Three each form joint ventures with Japanese automakers, displaying the foreign cars alongside US-made vehicles in their showrooms.

The Arab oil embargo ended on March 18, 1974, but it had a lasting impact on American society. While US automakers had begun making improvements to their compact cars and Japanese autos were rolling along American roads, these vehicles still ran on gasoline. It was time to begin looking for alternatives to fossil-based fuel.

Alternative Fuels

Owners of a Ford Model T could run their car on either gasoline or ethanol, also known as ethyl alcohol, the substance from which alcoholic beverages are made. Ethanol is a biofuel and can be made by fermenting several natural plant sources, including corn,

Biofuels like ethanol are made from plants such as sugarcane, being harvested here. Most automobile engines today can run on fuel containing no more than 10 percent ethanol.

potatoes, and sugarcane. Although gasoline became the main fuel for automobiles, Henry Ford still believed in alternative fuels, telling the *New York Times*, "The fuel of the future is going to come from fruit like that sumach out by the road, or from apples, weeds, sawdust—almost anything. There is fuel in every bit of vegetable matter that can be fermented."[35] While gasoline's low price and high energy level eventually made it the standard automotive fuel, ethanol saw a resurgence in popularity as a result of the Arab oil embargo.

In 1974 legislation was passed to promote research into the uses of solar energy, which included the possibility of using the sun to transform organic materials into fuel. The next year, the government began phasing out lead in gasoline, an additive that prevented damaging engine knocking. Petroleum producers added 2 percent ethanol to replace the lead, which helped eliminate some harmful emissions as well as reduced the amount of gas used. The discovery that another component of gasoline, MTBE, was contaminating groundwater supplies spurred further adoption of ethanol. Eventually, all automotive engines built in the United States were able to run on gasoline containing as much as 10 percent ethanol.

Diesel engines, which power the majority of trucks and buses (as well as some cars) on the road today, can operate on an alternative fuel called biodiesel. Made from renewable sources such as soybean oil or animal fats, biodiesel can be used alone or blended with petroleum-based diesel. According to a joint study by the US Department of Energy and the US Department of Agriculture, the use of biodiesel can reduce carbon dioxide emissions by 78 percent compared to petroleum-based diesel fuel. In 2016, 2.8 billion gallons (10.6 billion L) of biodiesel were sold. The goal of biodiesel producers is to garner 10 percent of the diesel fuel market by 2022.

Climate Change

In developing alternative fuels to alleviate the oil shortage, petroleum scientists also sought to reduce the harmful emissions that contribute to the problem of climate change, also known as global warming. Burning fossil fuels creates waste products called greenhouse gases that include, among other compounds, carbon dioxide. Carbon dioxide traps heat in the atmosphere, much like a greenhouse creates a warm climate in which plants can thrive. But when too much carbon dioxide is discharged into the atmosphere, it can have disastrous results: Glaciers melt, causing sea levels to rise; natural disasters such as hurricanes increase in intensity; and many animal and plant species can face extinction.

> "About a third of the total greenhouse gas emissions in the United States are from the transportation sector."[36]
>
> —Margo T. Oge, former EPA official

One of the main causes of climate change is the automobile. "Every gallon of gas or diesel," explains Margo T. Oge, former Transportation and Air Quality director at the US Environmental Protection Agency (EPA), "emits carbon dioxide, the greenhouse gas that accelerates climate change. As a result, about a third of the total greenhouse gas emissions in the United States are from the transportation sector."[36]

Although carbon dioxide is an invisible gas, other pollution pro-duced by auto exhaust was very easy to see and breathe. By the 1960s large American cities were feeling the effects of automotive emissions. One of the worst cities for automotive pollution was Los Angeles, California. In 1948 a chemist named Arie Haagen-Smit made the connection between automobile exhaust and the dense cloud of smog that continually plagued the city, causing eye irritation, respiratory problems, and even damage to crops.

Smog Hits Los Angeles

When the first cloud of smog hit Los Angeles, California, in July 1943, it was like a monster attacking the city straight out of a horror film. Chip Jacobs and William J. Kelly describe the scene in their book, *Smogtown*.

The beast you couldn't stab fanned its poison across the waking downtown. Cunning and silent, its gray mist engulfed buildings and streetcars, obscuring the sun and killing all sense of direction as it assaulted Los Angeles' citizenry with a face-stinging burn. Though nobody realized it then, the mystery cloud-bank would rattle the planet—making "green" a cause, not just a color—but first there was the suffering, a city full of it. Inhaling the viscous stuff socked folks with instant allergies whether they had them before or not, eyes welled, throats rasped, hands grasped for hankies and for answers. . . .

Peoples' attempted escapes from the noxious cloud bred hair-raising street drama. Blinded drivers jerked from side to side to avoid collisions. Mothers snatched up frightened children into ornate lobbies for shelter. If it was hard on pedestrians, it was hellish for the beat cops supervising public safety, let alone for any dangling window-washers. Whatever had summar-ily blanketed downtown was reminiscent of a harsh, pea-soup London fog. Then again, this was Southern California, where fabulous sunshine was a birthright. Try telling that to the beast.

Chip Jacobs and William J. Kelly, *Smogtown: The Lung-Burning History of Pollution in Los Angeles*. Woodstock, NY: Overlook, 2008, pp. 13–14.

In the 1950s and 1960s the city of Los Angeles had some of the most polluted air in the world. Heavy smog from vehicle exhaust saturates the air on this Los Angeles highway in 1954.

At first, Haagen-Smit's findings were rejected by the auto industry. "The Ford engineering staff," the automaker stated in 1953, "although mindful that automobile engines produce gases, feels that these waste vapors are dissipated in the atmosphere quickly and do not present an air pollution problem."[37] But in 1959 California established an agency to test cars and set pollution standards; soon thereafter, the automakers began equipping their cars with pollution-control devices. The positive crankcase ventilation valve, which limited gases escaping from the engine, was mandated for all new cars in California in 1961. By 1964 most US cars had them. In 1975 the US government required the installation of another pollution-control device, the catalytic converter. Placed in the exhaust system, the unit converts dangerous exhaust gases into less harmful compounds.

Unfortunately, while catalytic converters reduce smog and harmful gases called nitrogen oxides, they do not reduce the emission of carbon dioxide. Although these and other emission-control devices have helped make the air cleaner, the millions of cars and trucks on American roads are still a large contributor to the problem of global warming.

CHAPTER 4

Twenty-First-Century Automotive Technology

In 1911 Charles F. Kettering created an invention that would revolutionize the automobile. One of the most daunting tasks for early drivers was starting their car. A crank had to be inserted into the front of the automobile and then vigorously turned until the engine sputtered to life. This task was not without risks: If the engine backfired, it could spin the crank backward, seriously injuring the driver.

An industrial engineer, Kettering had adapted a small electric motor to open a cash register drawer with the push of a button. Henry M. Leland, developer of the Cadillac, hired Kettering to create a similar mechanism for starting his cars. Kettering's device, which started the engine by pushing a button on the dashboard, was incorporated into the 1912 Cadillac. It was an immediate success, and in less than ten years all cars had electric starters.

The convenience and safety of Kettering's starter contributed to the demise of the electric car, which had up to that point rivaled cars with internal combustion engines. Electric cars had been especially popular among women. Since it took a great deal of strength to crank a car, women preferred to drive easy-starting electric vehicles. But because of Kettering's invention, women soon began driving Fords, Cadillacs, and other gas-powered automobiles equipped with electric starters. "It was a complete game changer," says Greg Wallace, manager of GM's Heritage Center. "Within a few years, Cadillac featured women in their advertising showing them as drivers, instead of passengers or bystanders."[38] With the help of Kettering's invention, the internal combustion engine won the public's approval, and by 1920 production of electric cars ended.

Innovations like Kettering's electric starter have had a profound impact on the automobile industry and, in turn, on society. Such innovations continue to shape the automobile industry and have made cars safer, more reliable, more enjoyable to drive, and more environmentally friendly.

The Electric Car Returns

When the original electric cars disappeared in the early twentieth century, few people could have predicted that the technology would experience a resurgence more than seventy years later. In 1996 a new car unlike any other appeared on the road. The EV1, created by GM, was the first modern electric vehicle made available to the public. Powered by lead-acid batteries, the EV1 could travel 55 to 95 miles (88.5 to 153 km) between charges and attain a maximum speed of 80 miles per hour (129 kph).

The EV1 was a new and untested concept, designed to let motorists test-drive the cars and give their opinions to GM. Despite positive feedback, however, GM ultimately declared that an electric car was not economically viable, although some say GM was afraid that the EV1 would adversely affect sales of its main product, internal combustion engine vehicles. GM officially canceled the program in 2003 and destroyed all but a handful of EV1s.

Although GM abandoned electric vehicles, an entrepreneur named Elon Musk saw them as the future of automotive technology. Musk's company, Tesla Motors (named for inventor and electric power visionary Nikola Tesla), had a single goal: to "accelerate the advent of sustainable transport by bringing compelling mass-market electric cars to the market as soon as possible."[39]

In 2006 Musk unveiled the Tesla Roadster, a sleek electric sports car powered by a lithium-ion battery. The two-seat

A Tesla Model S powers up at a charging station. Electric vehicles rely on an onboard battery that produces no emissions.

Roadster could travel nearly 250 miles (402 km) between charges and accelerate from 0 to 60 miles per hour (97 kph) in under four seconds. "What was unique about the Roadster," says Musk, "was it was the first really great electric car. And before the Roadster, people thought an electric car would be slow and ugly and low range and have bad performance. And we had to break that mold."[40]

Around 2,450 of the sleek automobiles were sold before the model was discontinued in 2012. That same year Tesla created the Model S sedan, and in 2017 it began marketing the Model 3, a smaller, more affordable electric car. Other manufacturers soon joined the emerging electric car revolution. In 2010 Nissan introduced the Leaf, a low-priced compact electric with an initial range of 107 miles (172 km). By 2017 Ford, Chevrolet, BMW,

Honda, Mercedes-Benz, and other auto factories were turning out electric cars.

While these wholly electric cars are environmentally friendly, many people are wary about giving up the proven reliability of internal combustion power. For them, hybrid cars bridge the gap between electric and gasoline engines.

Hybrid Power

As electric automobiles were beginning to reappear in the late 1990s, their drawbacks—high initial cost, limited range, and lack of roadside charging stations—led some carmakers to consider another option: the hybrid vehicle. A hybrid uses both a gasoline engine and an electric motor. There are several types of hybrids that are distinguished by the way the two power sources are utilized. A full hybrid can use either gasoline or electric power (or a combination of both) to drive the vehicle. A partial hybrid uses its electric motor to assist the gas engine for better economy but cannot drive the car by itself. A plug-in hybrid relies mainly on its electric motor to propel the vehicle, with the gasoline engine used to extend the driving range. Unlike the full and partial hybrids, as its name suggests, the plug-in hybrid can be connected to a special electric outlet to recharge its batteries.

> "The Prius blazed a path for every other clean car."[41]
>
> —Ben Stewart, journalist

The Toyota Prius, which arrived in the United States in 2000, became the first successful hybrid car in America and eventually the most popular hybrid worldwide. "The Toyota Prius is the granddaddy of all green machines," says automotive journalist Ben Stewart. "No other car is more closely tied to fuel-efficient technology than the Prius. . . . The Prius blazed a path for every other clean car."[41]

A full hybrid, the Prius is powered at low speeds by its electric motor. When cruising at highway speeds, the gasoline engine takes over, and both sources are used when more power

Tesla's Gigafactory

All electric cars need batteries to run. While it takes a small battery to operate a flashlight or cell phone, electric cars require large, heavy, expensive batteries. This is why electric car manufacturer Tesla is creating its own factory to economically build the batteries needed for its vehicles.

Construction on the Tesla Gigafactory began in 2014 in the Nevada desert near Reno and as of January 2018, is still in progress. At about 5.5 million square feet (510,967 sq m) in 2017, phase 1 is the largest building in the world, with a projected final-phase area of 13 million square feet (1.2 million sq m) when completed. By 2020 it will employ about sixty-five hundred workers. The first phase of the Gigafactory opened on July 29, 2016.

In January 2017 mass production of lithium-ion batteries for the various Tesla models began at the Gigafactory, in partnership with Japanese electronics giant Panasonic. When the Gigafactory is running at full capacity, it will be able to build as many batteries in one year as were made globally in 2013. This will allow Tesla to manufacture about 1.5 million cars a year. A new Gigafactory for making batteries and Tesla cars is being planned for construction in Europe.

The factory's name comes from the prefix *giga*, meaning "billion," a reflection of Elon Musk's big environmental vision. For him, the Gigafactory is "about being able to make enough electric cars . . . that it actually moves the needle from a global carbon production perspective—so that it actually does really change the world. It has to be big because the world is big."

Quoted in Jessica Easto, ed., *Rocket Man: Elon Musk in His Own Words*. Chicago: Agate, 2017, p. 65.

is needed during acceleration. This arrangement, which Toyota calls Hybrid Synergy Drive, gives the car a combined city/highway economy rating of up to 56 miles per gallon (23.8 km/L). The Prius also saves energy by using a system called regenerative braking, which recaptures some of the kinetic energy generated by the brakes when stopping and uses it to recharge the battery.

In 2004 Chevrolet, Ford, and Honda entered the hybrid arena with new hybrid models of existing vehicles. "All new cars will have some degree of hybridization by 2020," Chuck Squatriglia, story editor at *Wired* magazine, predicted in 2008. "Battery technology will be ubiquitous and vehicles will communicate with one another and the road to make driving safer and easier."[42] Given the advantages of electric and hybrid cars, that prediction appears to be headed toward reality.

Electric and Hybrid Impact

The most obvious, and most important, impact of these new vehicles is their effect on the environment. As government standards for automobile emissions tightened in the 1990s and early 2000s, electric and hybrid vehicles became the front line in the fight against automotive pollution. In 2017 the EPA, in conjunction with the National Highway Transportation Safety Administration (NHTSA), set a target of 54.5 miles per gallon (23 km/L) for all passenger cars and light-duty trucks by 2025, an increase from 35.5 miles per gallon (15 km/L) in 2016. According to the EPA, this new standard "conserves billions of barrels of oil, cuts carbon pollution, protects consumer choice, and enables long-term planning for automakers."[43]

"Vehicles will communicate with one another and the road to make driving safer and easier."[42]

—Chuck Squatriglia, story editor, *Wired* magazine

Of course, the electricity to charge all-electric vehicles or plug-in hybrids comes from power plants, and more than 60 percent of them in the United States are run by fossil fuels (coal, natural gas, and petroleum). This means that the positive environmental effect of electric cars that derive their power from certain sources is limited. As science journalist Nicholas Gerbis explains:

The electrical production process has a significant impact: According to one study, lifetime greenhouse gas emissions from plug-in hybrids come out to about one-third less than those put out by traditional gasoline-powered cars, but using coal-fired electricity, they have a worse carbon footprint than traditional gas-electric hybrids, although they still beat out traditional cars. Experts project that coal plants will constitute the major source of electricity through 2035.[44]

In urban environments, where pollution is the worst, electric vehicles are helping reduce smog and other environmental pollutants. Delivery trucks, buses, US Postal Service vehicles, and taxicabs all make frequent stops and starts and spend a good deal of time idling. In this kind of driving, internal combustion engines create more pollution than they do when traveling on highways. Electric and hybrid power, as well as other more environmentally friendly fuels such as propane and natural gas, are being used to reduce the emissions in cities around the world.

Jammed urban streets and highways force drivers to make frequent stops and idle their engines. This produces more emissions than driving on the open road. One solution might be to make common transports—such as delivery trucks and taxis—reliant on electric or hybrid engines.

Electric vehicles run not only cleanly but quietly, too. "No one wants to have the idling noise and diesel fumes in their neighborhood," remarks Charles Freese of GM. "It would be great if the only sign that a delivery company was there would be the ring of your doorbell and the package left on your porch."[45] On the other hand, the almost noiseless operation of electric vehicles can be hazardous to pedestrians, especially those with hearing impairments, who may not perceive an electric vehicle approaching. Says US secretary of transportation Anthony Foxx, "We all depend on our senses to alert us to possible danger. With more, quieter hybrid and electrical cars on the road, the ability for all pedestrians to hear as well as see the cars becomes an important factor of reducing the risk of possible crashes and improving safety."[46]

An NHTSA study found that pedestrians are 37 percent more likely to be involved in an accident with hybrid or electric cars than traditional vehicles. Federal safety standards now require electric vehicles to emit a sound when going less than 19 miles per hour (30.6 kph). External speakers in the front or rear of the car can emit sounds to warn pedestrians of its approach, with a variety of sounds that may someday be downloaded like ringtones.

Modern technology has created cleaner, more fuel-efficient cars. But perhaps even more important to the everyday driver, it has also made cars smarter and safer to drive.

Sensing the World

Ever since the early twentieth century, when automobiles first appeared on city streets and country roads, drivers have mainly relied on two of the five human senses—sight and hearing—to operate their vehicles. In the early twenty-first century, however, those senses alone seem inadequate for navigating the speed limits of interstate highways or the congestion of city streets. So automakers have supplemented our human senses with a variety of electronic sensors built into the latest cars.

Today's automobiles have an average of sixty to one hundred sensors, and the sensor industry predicts the number may rise to as many as two hundred as cars get even more high-tech. Many of these sensors work quietly behind the scenes to monitor and control the engine, exhaust system, brakes, and other critical components. These types of sensors have been a part of the typical automobile for years. But the newest sensors use the latest in detection technology to help drivers operate the vehicle safely for both its occupants and other drivers and pedestrians.

Avoiding Collisions

Traffic accidents are a major cause of injury, death, and property damage in the United States. The NHTSA has estimated that there were more than 6 million crashes reported to police in 2015. The number is certainly higher if minor, nonreported accidents are included. Of these accidents, more than 40 percent are rear-end collisions, which happen on average about every eight seconds. Technology known variously as collision avoidance, forward-collision warning, or pre-collision systems can help reduce such accidents. Jon Linkov of *Consumer Reports* explains how collision avoidance works:

> These cutting-edge active safety systems rely on a number of sensors, cameras, lasers, and short- and long-range radar. They monitor what is going on around the vehicle—vehicles, pedestrians, cyclists, and even road signs—as well as the vehicle itself. Inputs are processed by computers, which then prompt some action from the car or the driver. Those actions may start with attention-grabbers, such as a beep, a flashing dashboard icon, a tug from the seatbelt, or a vibration in the seat or steering wheel. If the driver doesn't respond, the more advanced systems then apply partial or full braking force.[47]

A car can also cause accidents should it drift from its lane. Modern cars are therefore equipped with lane-departure warnings that monitor lane markings and alert the driver to counteract the drift,

Dangerous Designs

The modern advances that automobile designers build into the latest cars make it safer, simpler, and more intuitive to operate a vehicle. Sometimes, however, a seemingly good design can have unexpected flaws.

One of the newest advances is the electronic shifter. Instead of a standard shift lever, an electronic shifter changes gears with a slight movement of a knob located on the center console. It is easy to operate and provides a modern design element. The designers anticipated that the knob would be intuitive to operate, but instead it caused confusion for many drivers. Unlike a standard shifter, where the driver can tell by look or feel which gear the vehicle is in, the knob provides little tactile feedback to indicate the selected gear. A driver may think the car is in one gear when it is actually in another. Such confusion can have deadly results.

In 2016 *Star Trek* actor Anton Yelchin was killed when his idling vehicle rolled forward, pinning him against a gate outside his home. Investigators looked at the electronic shifter as a likely cause of the accident. Eventually, 1.1 million vehicles were recalled, including the model that killed Yelchin, to fix the shifter problem.

Automotive engineers have a daunting responsibility. While they strive to make new cars better and safer, they must also be sure that what looks good on the drawing board does not create problems in real-life situations.

or even command the car to make that correction automatically. Similar systems use cameras to detect whether another car is in the driver's blind spot, where the view of traffic to the side of the car is limited. Warnings or automatic corrections take place to keep the cars from colliding. Many other sensors in and around the car help make driving safer. Rear-mounted backup cameras, which allow drivers to see areas behind the car that are not visible through the rear window, became standard equipment in 2018. Sensors can warn a driver of traffic approaching from either side when reversing, sense when a pedestrian is about to walk into a vehicle's path, help the driver park the car, warn a driver that he or she is getting drowsy, and even start the windshield wipers when rain is detected.

Driving a Computer

All these sensors require significant computer power to work. The first computer was installed in an automobile in 1968 when Volkswagen introduced a computer-controlled fuel injection system into some of its models. Since then, the automotive computer has grown significantly; twenty-first-century cars can have from twenty-five to fifty central processing units (CPUs), the electronic brain found inside all computers. Of course, all of these computers need software to work. "Mainstream cars," says technology consultant Bob O'Donnell, "may have up to 10 million lines of code and high-end luxury sedans can have nearly 100 million—that's about 14 times more than even a Boeing 787 Dreamliner jet."[48]

The myriad of electronic sensors and CPUs present in today's cars impacts more than just safety and the environment; it also affects design and demand. Potential car buyers want more electronics in their vehicles, which pushes manufacturers to comply with their customers' wishes. The more electronics that are installed in cars, the lower the prices of components such as touch screens can be, allowing better technology at more competitive prices. And as electronics creates safer cars, insurance companies will feel the impact as well. According to Alastair Hayfield of consulting firm IHS Markit, "Electronics are changing how vehicles are designed, built and driven. They are shaping companies' business models—and customers' buying decisions."[49]

> "Electronics are changing how vehicles are designed, built and driven."[49]
>
> —Alastair Hayfield, business consultant

But can cars come with too much technology? Some studies have shown that the more technology a car has, the worse a person's driving skills can get. This is because drivers may rely too much on automated systems to do the driving, instead of using them as backups for their own abilities. Indeed, some drivers may use electronics as substitutes for their own attention to their surroundings. Drivers may also get distracted by the many things a modern car can do. The

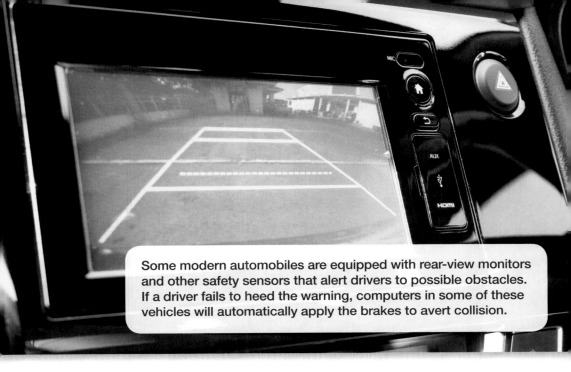

Some modern automobiles are equipped with rear-view monitors and other safety sensors that alert drivers to possible obstacles. If a driver fails to heed the warning, computers in some of these vehicles will automatically apply the brakes to avert collision.

so-called infotainment systems—which use a touch screen in the dashboard to provide the driver with information for satellite navigation, radio, and other music systems—along with text or phone communication, can be a major source of driver distraction. According to a government report, taking one's eyes off the road for just two seconds doubles the risk of having an accident. Using the navigation function can be particularly hazardous. A study conducted by the American Automobile Association and the University of Utah found that "destination entry for navigation took an average of 40 seconds. . . . At 25 mph drivers would travel just under 1,500 feet while using the [navigation system] for entering destinations, and several of the navigation systems that were tested took considerably longer than the 40-second average."[50]

Despite all the cutting-edge technology in today's cars, drivers need to be especially attentive to the task of driving when they are behind the wheel, where a distraction of mere seconds can be fatal. But with the rapid pace at which automotive technology is accelerating, perhaps driving skills will become less important in the future, where fully autonomous, self-driving cars are destined to be the biggest innovation since the Model T.

A New Automotive Age

In 1956 an automotive extravaganza sponsored by GM opened in New York City, the first stop on a five-city tour. The show, dubbed Motorama, was a touring exhibition in which GM presented its latest prototypes and concept cars to the public. The crowds at Motorama were impressed by the Buicks, Cadillacs, and Oldsmobiles on display, but the car that most stirred their imagination looked more like a jet plane than an automobile.

With a streamlined body, vertical tail fin, clear bubble canopy, and gas turbine engine, the Firebird II was a glimpse into the possible future of the automobile. Along with its futuristic lines and unique power source the Firebird II had another intriguing detail: It was designed to travel along "the highway of tomorrow" without the need for a driver. According to the Firebird II's brochure, "This amazing concept places control of the motorcar in the hands of an 'electronic brain'—actually releasing the driver from the wheel."[51]

In this early idea for an autonomous, or self-driving, car, the Firebird II was only one piece of an elaborate system. It was imagined that antennas in the front of the car would sense a magnetic strip in the road to keep the vehicle on course, and a series of roadside control towers, manned by human operators, would communicate with the driver to assure that everything ran smoothly. As a concept car, designed to showcase its cutting-edge designs, the Firebird II never went into production. But even though the idea of cars following strips embedded into highways was impractical, the idea of an autonomous car never entirely went away. By the twenty-first century, such a vehicle was not only possible, it was all but inevitable.

Modern Driverless Cars

In March 2015 a blue 2014 Audi SQ5 rolled into New York City at the end of a 3,400-mile (5,472 km) cross-country trip. What made the journey remarkable was the fact that for 99 percent of the time, no human touched the controls. Radar, laser sensors, and numerous cameras kept the car en route and driving at the posted speed limit. Only when the car entered construction zones or congested urban environments did the human driver intervene. "We expected we would be in autonomous mode most of the time," says Jeff Owens, chief technology officer of Delphi, the company that conducted the trip, "but to be in it close to 99 percent of the time was a pleasant surprise. . . . This technology has come so far."[52]

Internet giant Google has also adopted autonomous vehicle technology in its own driverless car initiative. Begun in 2009, the project was spun off as an independent company called Waymo in 2016. Using Prius, Audi, and Lexus vehicles fitted with $150,000 worth of navigation equipment, Waymo tested its concept first on highways, then in more congested city streets filled with hazards such as bicyclists, pedestrians, and drivers opening the doors of their parked cars into the traffic flow. By June 2016 the Waymo autonomous vehicle fleet had driven a total of 1,725,911 miles (2,777,585 km).

> "[The Firebird II] places control of the motorcar in the hands of an 'electronic brain'—actually releasing the driver from the wheel."[51]
>
> —A 1956 GM promotional brochure

Waymo soon progressed from fitting standard vehicles with radar and lasers to building an autonomous car from the ground up. "It was a big decision for us to go and start building our first purpose-built vehicles," says Chris Urmson, director of Google self-driving cars. "And really they're prototype vehicles. They were a chance for us to explore: what does it really mean to have a self-driving vehicle."[53] The resulting car, nicknamed Firefly, was a small, two-seat electric vehicle shaped roughly like a four-wheeled egg. Its many navigation devices included a 360-degree laser sensor in a dome atop the car.

The Firefly's interior was remarkable for what it did not have: There were no accelerator or brake pedals and no steering wheel. The only way the car could be driven was autonomously. This was a decided advantage for Steve Mahan, who took a ride in the Firefly. "I've never been in Austin, Texas," Mahan commented during the journey, "and now I'm driving in Austin, Texas." Riding

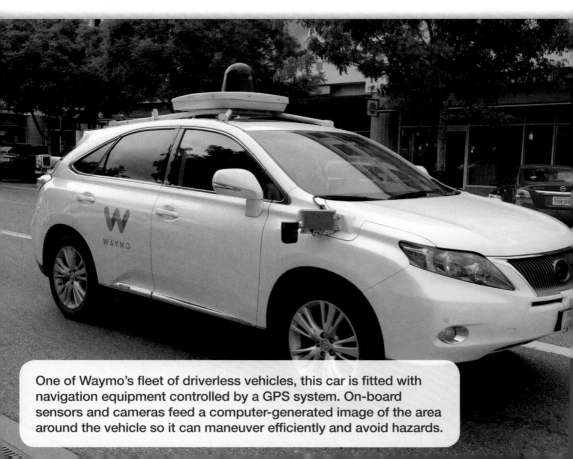

One of Waymo's fleet of driverless vehicles, this car is fitted with navigation equipment controlled by a GPS system. On-board sensors and cameras feed a computer-generated image of the area around the vehicle so it can maneuver efficiently and avoid hazards.

might be a better word than driving, because Mahan is blind. It was the first time he had been in a car by himself in twelve years. "It's a profound experience for me to be alone in the car. A very important segment of my life was cut away when my vision failed. And a self-driving car would give me a huge part of my life back."[54]

For people with physical disabilities like Mahan, or the elderly who can no longer safely drive, an autonomous car can provide the opportunity to perform ordinary tasks, such as shopping, or enjoy social activities, such as visiting family and friends. While these are a few of the clearly life-changing benefits of autonomous automobiles, two major questions loom over the coming age of the driverless car: Are they secure, and are they safe?

Beware of Hackers

Autonomous cars rely on a multitude of computers in order to navigate in traffic, respond to potential hazards, and keep the vehicle on course to its destination. But as anyone who uses a computer can attest, these versatile devices are vulnerable to viruses, software glitches, and perhaps most dangerous of all, malicious hackers.

Andy Greenberg found out firsthand what hackers can do to a car. Driving at 70 miles per hour (112.6 kph) in St. Louis, Missouri, Greenberg's vehicle suddenly began acting up. He explains:

> Though I hadn't touched the dashboard, the vents in the Jeep Cherokee started blasting cold air at the maximum setting, chilling the sweat on my back through the in-seat climate control system. Next the radio switched to the local hip hop station and began blaring Skee-lo at full volume. I spun the control knob left and hit the power button, to no avail. Then the windshield wipers turned on, and wiper fluid blurred the glass.[55]

Hackers had taken over some of the functions of Greenberg's Jeep, but at first he was not unduly alarmed; in fact, he was part of an experiment conducted by researchers Charlie Miller and Chris Valasek. "The Jeep's strange behavior wasn't entirely unexpected," he admits. "I'd come to St. Louis to be Miller and Valasek's digital crash-test dummy, a willing subject on whom they could test the car-hacking research they'd been doing over the past year."[56]

Hijacking a car's climate-control system and radio may have seemed relatively harmless to Greenberg, but soon the experiment took a scarier turn. The hackers disabled the Jeep's transmission. "Immediately my accelerator stopped working," Greenberg recalls. "This occurred just as I reached a long overpass, with no shoulder to offer an escape. The experiment had ceased to be fun."[57] Soon the hackers disabled the Jeep's brakes, leaving Greenberg frantically pumping the useless brake pedal as the Jeep skidded into a ditch.

As Greenberg learned, hacking a car is no game; it can lead to serious injury or even death. Miller and Valasek are actually two of the good guys, "white hat" hackers who use their skills to uncover flaws in software. They found a loophole in the car's entertainment system that allowed them to wirelessly manipulate the system. Fiat Chrysler, Jeep's parent company, recalled 1.4 million non-self-driving Cherokees in order to fix the defect in the software. But thousands of vehicles made by other manufacturers incorporate similar wireless systems, which may also have weaknesses that make them vulnerable to a hacker attack.

As cars become more computerized and Internet-connected, finding and fixing vulnerabilities has become a priority. In 2015 auto industry companies established the Automotive Information Sharing and Analysis Center to analyze vehicle cybersecurity risks and share such information among its members. In March 2017 Senators Edward Markey and Richard Blumenthal introduced legislation to combat the hacking threat. The Security and Privacy in Your Car Act, if passed into law, would require the NHTSA to set standards for automobile security to combat hackers. "This critical legislation will help protect the public against cybercrimi-

Are Self-Driving Cars Too Easy to Trick?

Contrary to popular belief, it does not take a computer expert to hack an autonomous vehicle. Researchers at the University of Washington have figured out a very simple way to confuse the cameras that help autonomous vehicles identify objects in the surrounding environment—and in doing so have exposed a potential danger associated with self-driving cars.

The cameras send images to the car's computer system, which has been programmed to recognize everyday objects such as people, traffic lights, and road signs. When a sign is detected, the computer must figure out what it says, and therein lies the system's weakness.

Using an ordinary computer printer, the researchers discovered two ways to mislead a car's visual identification system. They printed out several small rectangular black-and-white shapes and stuck them to a standard stop sign, which fooled the computer into thinking it was a speed limit sign. Such a trick deceives the car's system while remaining inconspicuous to human drivers, who may think they are simply seeing graffiti. In another test, the self-driving car was fooled by a full-size, specially printed sign that was placed over an existing directional sign.

The consequences of such trickery are obvious. A car that does not recognize a stop sign can speed through an intersection, potentially causing a deadly accident. It is clear that automakers must prepare to make self-driving cars immune not only to sophisticated cyberhackers, but also malicious pranksters whose only weapon is an inexpensive printer.

nals," says Blumenthal, "who exploit advances in technology like wireless connected . . . self-driving cars. Security and safety cannot be sacrificed as we achieve the convenience and promise of wireless progress."[58] Auto manufacturers are also concerned about computer security, hiring white hat hackers to ferret out bugs in their own autonomous software.

How Safe Are Autonomous Cars?

As manufacturers and the government work to improve vehicle cybersecurity, the quest to achieve safe driverless automobiles is being played out on the streets of America. By the end of 2015, Waymo vehicles had driven more than 4 million miles (6.4 million km) with only one at-fault accident—a modified Lexus SUV traveling at 2 miles per hour (3.2 kph) hit the side of a bus.

While tapping a bus at a walking pace does not sound all that significant, more serious accidents are bound to occur. An autonomous vehicle's sensors provide one source of potential problems. A car's cameras can be blinded by dirt, ice, or glare. Fog, snow, or heavy rain can make laser sensors unreliable. And while radar beams are good at detecting solid objects, they can become confused when bouncing off structures such as bridges and tunnels.

Autonomous vehicles are still in their infancy. While on-board computers might ably detect people and objects nearby, designers have not resolved how the autos will react in all situations, especially those that require choosing to avoid one accident in favor of causing another.

All these sensors need the power of artificial intelligence (AI) behind them to translate the data collected into signals that control the car. But how AI reacts to various situations depends on the people who program it. With humans providing the computer code, the term *artificial* can be a bit misleading. "There is nothing artificial about intelligence," says AI consultant Kartik Iyengar. "Replacing adaptive human behavior with rigid, artificial intelligence could cause irrational behavior within ecosystems of people and things."[59]

Autonomous cars must make millions of split-second decisions about data received from their sensors. But there is an ethical aspect to those decisions. For example, how should a vehicle react to a group of people that appears in its path? It could slam on the brakes, but that could injure the car's passengers or cause a rear-end collision. It might swerve to the right, but perhaps there is a child playing on the sidewalk; a swerve to the left may crash the car into a building. Resolving this moral dilemma would be difficult even for a human. Is the life of a child more valuable than a group of adults? Should the car's passengers, who have no say in the situation, be sacrificed to avoid a greater loss of life? These difficult questions will continue to confront the programmers who must decide what the autonomous vehicles will do in any situation.

The question of autonomous vehicle safety is difficult to answer with any certainty. Automotive safety statistics are based on accidents occurring over a long period. One study estimated that it would take data from hundreds of millions of miles of autonomous driving over "tens or even hundreds of years"[60] to gather meaningful information about the cars' safety. But even without hard data, Ryan Hagemann, an auto robotics specialist at think tank TechFreedom, thinks that autonomous cars will be safer than today's human-controlled vehicles. "In theory," he notes, "if you have 100 percent fully autonomous vehicles on the road . . . you're basically looking at anywhere from a 95 to 99.99 percent reduction in total fatalities and injuries on the road."[61]

The Autonomous Future

What might it be like to go for a car ride in the future? Margo T. Oge, who headed the EPA's Office of Transportation and Air Quality, imagines such a scenario in her book *Driving the Future*.

On September 30, 2040, a slight woman in jeans and a T-shirt swipes off her e-book and steps out of a silently idling car on a busy street. "Park Mode," she says and then watches as the empty, single-occupant car pulls down to the entrance of the parking garage underneath her apartment building. . . .

The car's surface still glows in the woman's favorite shade of purple. The color-changing exterior also acts as a solar panel that powers the air conditioning and accessories when the vehicle is idling in traffic. The car's body contains no steel, but is constructed primarily out of aluminum and plastics, weighing in at about 1,650 pounds. The electric engine gets about 100 miles per gallon (mpg), close to the global average, and puts out zero emissions. . . .

The car's navigation system has helped it travel 120,000 miles without so much as a scratch, but the technology also helps the car quickly find a parking space in the darkened garage. Four low-light cameras integrated into the frame guide it into a cramped space between two other vehicles. The car's exterior fades back to its default blue shade, and it begins wirelessly powering up for the next customer.

Margo T. Oge, *Driving the Future: Combating Climate Change with Cleaner, Smarter Cars.* New York: Arcade, 2015, pp. 1–2.

Such a bold prediction may or may not become reality, but automakers are working to make self-driving cars safer than nonautonomous vehicles. When that happens, the roles of auto owner and driver will undergo a major transformation.

A New World

Industry visionaries have long speculated about the impact that new automotive technologies would have on future society. "Exactly what that world might look like is anybody's guess," says Eric Tingwall of *Car and Driver* magazine. "The computer-driven car could make America's most congested roads flow freely for the first time in decades, or it could stress our infrastructure to collapse."[62] As unknowable as this future world might be, experts attempt to predict the trends that autonomous electric vehicles will create.

Some predict that the advent of autonomous vehicles will spell the end of individual automobile ownership. Uber, the popular ride-sharing company, has provided on-demand car transportation since it began in 2009; the company recorded its billionth ride in 2015. The next year, Uber began adding self-driving cars to its fleets in several states, including Pennsylvania and Arizona. Self-driving cars provided by companies like Uber and its competitor, Lyft, may make car ownership—and its attendant costs for fuel, maintenance, and insurance—obsolete. A 2017 study by research firm RethinkX agrees and paints a remarkable picture of the future:

> "We are on the cusp of one of the fastest, deepest, most consequential disruptions of transportation in history."[63]
>
> —James Arbib and Tony Seba, automotive researchers, RethinkX

> We are on the cusp of one of the fastest, deepest, most consequential disruptions of transportation in history. By 2030 . . . 95% of U.S. passenger miles traveled will be served by on-demand autonomous electric vehicles owned by fleets, not individuals. [This] will have enormous implications across the transportation and oil industries, decimating entire portions of their value chains, causing oil demand and prices to plummet, and destroying trillions of dollars in investor value—but also creating trillions of dollars in new business opportunities.[63]

Cities will radically change as autonomous vehicles multiply. According to Tingwall, cities may be crowded with "hordes of robocars idly circling our streets or, more likely, retreating to storage yards at the edges of our cities"[64] while their owners are at work. Accidents will be rare as advanced sensors keep the cars from colliding with pedestrians, bicyclists, and other vehicles. Even the air quality will improve as electric cars supplant internal combustion vehicles.

Unused parking lots in urban environments might be repurposed as parks or playgrounds or used for housing and new businesses. More trees and grassy areas will add aesthetic beauty to cities, as well as create environments that are pedestrian friendly. The suburbs could see a rise in population and expand even farther from city centers. The daily commute will no longer be wasted hours; according to automotive research director David Muyres, the autonomous car will instead become a "living room on wheels,"[65] where passengers can read, watch videos, or just sit and relax. Businesses using autonomous delivery trucks will experience reduced shipping costs, lower fleet maintenance, and speedier deliveries, which will result in increased customer satisfaction.

This picture of an idyllic future is not without its drawbacks. As more autonomous cars and trucks ply the nation's streets and highways, many people may find themselves out of work. Gas station attendants, taxi drivers, and long-haul truckers may all find themselves in the unemployment line. Even without being hacked, an autonomous car's computer could suffer a software glitch, causing the vehicle to act erratically, shut down, or even accelerate out of control. Insurance companies will need to come up with new guidelines for determining fault in an accident, and government agencies will need to adapt current laws or create new ones to regulate the autonomous vehicle.

To Own or Not to Own

In the future will anyone really want to own an autonomous car? Getting more use from a car may be one way automobile ownership could change. Since most cars sit idle some 94 percent of the time, an owner could rent his or her car to others during that downtime. Multiple ownership systems may also develop, whereby several people own a share in an autonomous vehicle and use an app to call up the car when needed.

Some technology experts predict that autonomous vehicles will soon make commutes comfortable and stress-free. They foresee a world in which passengers can read, relax, or even conduct business while their driverless vehicles shuttle them around.

Economic and other practical reasons may favor a ride-sharing economy. But there is still that sense of independence people feel, or want to feel, when getting behind the wheel. "Car ownership is woven into the fabric of American life," remarks automotive entrepreneur Ale Resnik. "The majority of drivers see the cabin of their car as a personal space they treasure—and don't want to give up. So car ownership is here to stay, even when autonomous vehicles go mainstream."[66] A 2016 survey by research firm AutoPacific reported that "56 percent of respondents stated that they simply love driving and therefore would never give it up, while nearly half said that driverless cars would take all the fun out of driving."[67]

> "The majority of drivers see the cabin of their car as a personal space they treasure—and don't want to give up."[66]
>
> —Ale Resnik, automotive entrepreneur

The advent of the electric-powered, autonomous vehicle is the latest in a century of automotive milestones and one that is poised to change everything once more. Bold predictions about this new world—in which driving has become an obsolete skill, most people do not own cars, and the environment is cleaner than it has been in decades—may or may not come true. In the meantime, the world as we know it will keep turning on the wheels of one of the most influential inventions of all time: the automobile.

SOURCE NOTES

Introduction: A Revolution in Transportation

1. Jim Rasenberger, *America 1908: The Dawn of Flight, the Race to the Pole, the Invention of the Model T, and the Making of a Modern Nation*. New York: Scribner, 2007, p. 2.
2. Raymond Loewy, "Jukebox on Wheels," *Atlantic*, April 1955. www.theatlantic.com.

Chapter 1: Inventing the Horseless Carriage

3. Quoted in David M. Young, "A Mist Is as Good as a Mile," *Chicago Tribune*, April 1, 2007. www.chicago tribune.com.
4. Quoted in Byron Olsen and Joseph Cabadas, *The American Auto Factory*. St. Paul, MN: MBI, 2002, p. 14.
5. Henry Ford, *My Life and Work*. New York: Classic House, 2009, p. 18.
6. Douglas Brinkley, *Wheels for the World: Henry Ford, His Company, and a Century of Progress*. New York: Viking, 2003, p. 23.
7. Ford, *My Life and Work*, p. 55.
8. Ford, *My Life and Work*, p. 61.
9. Quoted in Brinkley, *Wheels for the World*, p. 153.
10. Ford, *My Life and Work*, p. 62.
11. Tony Swan, "Ford's Assembly Line Turns 100: How It Really Put the World on Wheels," *Car and Driver*, April 2013. www.caranddriver.com.
12. Quoted in *New York Daily News*, "Ford's Assembly Line Turns 100: How It Changed Society," October 7, 2013. www.nydailynews.com.
13. Quoted in Mark Lelinwalla, "Ford Shows How Humans and Robots Work Hand-in-Hand on Its Assembly Line," TechCrunch, July 14, 2016. www .techcrunch.com.

14. Quoted in *Wired*, *The Window: Tesla Model S*, YouTube. https://www.youtube.com/watch?v=8_lfxPI5ObM&list=PL1FlYvcyb28_wzenJzrrgkVU1xAcNcT4p.

15. Quoted in Brinkley, *Wheels for the World*, pp. 180–81.

Chapter 2: The Indispensable Automobile

16. Quoted in Jesse Snyder, "No New Cars, but That Didn't Stop US Automakers, Dealers During WWII," *Automotive News*, October 31, 2011. www.autonews.com.

17. Quoted in Kevin Ransom, "Tail Fins: Six Things You Didn't Know About the Iconic Automotive Shape," *Autoblog*, August 8, 2009. www.autoblog.com.

18. Quoted in Ransom, "Tail Fins."

19. Ford, *My Life and Work*, p. 55.

20. Harley Earl, "The Secret of Making Beautiful Cars in the 1950s," *Saturday Evening Post*, September 24, 2010. www.saturdayeveningpost.com.

21. Quoted in James J. Flink, *The Automobile Age*. Cambridge, MA: MIT Press, 1988, p. 293.

22. Dwight D. Eisenhower, *The White House Years: Mandate for Change, 1953–1956*. Garden City, NY: Doubleday, 1963, pp. 548–49.

23. Quoted in Dan McNichol, *The Roads That Built America: The Incredible Story of the U.S. Interstate System*. New York: Sterling, 2006, p. 154.

24. Catherine Lutz and Anne Lutz Fernandez, *Carjacked: The Culture of the Automobile and Its Effect on Our Lives*. New York: Palgrave Macmillan, 2010, p. 15.

Chapter 3: Crisis at the Pump

25. Quoted in Andrew Scott Cooper, *The Oil Kings: How the U.S., Iran, and Saudi Arabia Changed the Balance of Power in the Middle East.* New York: Simon & Schuster, 2011, p. 120.

26. Thomas Borstelmann, *The 1970s: A New Global History from Civil Rights to Economic Equality*. Princeton, NJ: Princeton University Press, 2012, p. 56.

27. Richard Nixon, "The Energy Emergency," *Weekly Compilation of Presidential Documents*, November 7, 1973, pp. 1,312–13.

28. Quoted in Meg Jacobs, *Panic at the Pump: The Energy Crisis and the Transformation of American Politics in the 1970s*. New York: Hill and Wang, 2016, p. 5.
29. Quoted in Cooper, *The Oil Kings*, p. 151.
30. Quoted in Robert Lindsey, "The Angry Truck Driver: 'We've Got to Show 'Em,'" *New York Times*, December 5, 1973. www.nytimes.com.
31. Quoted in Lindsey, "The Angry Truck Driver."
32. Quoted in Jacobs, *Panic at the Pump*, p. 90.
33. Richard Nixon, "Statement on Signing the Emergency Highway Energy Conservation Act," American Presidency Project. www.presidency.ucsb.edu.
34. Peter Cheney, "The Rise of Japan: How the Car Industry Was Won," *Toronto Globe and Mail*, November 5, 2015. www.theglobeandmail.com.
35. Quoted in Daniel Strohl, "Fact Check: Henry Ford Didn't Design the Model T as a Multi-Fuel Vehicle," *Hemmings Daily*, April 23, 2017. www.hemmings.com.
36. Margo T. Oge, *Driving the Future: Combating Climate Change with Cleaner, Smarter Cars*. New York: Arcade, 2015, p. 6.
37. Quoted in Jack Doyle, *Taken for a Ride: Detroit's Big Three and the Politics of Pollution*. New York: Four Walls Eight Windows, 2000, p. 17.

Chapter 4: Twenty-First-Century Automotive Technology

38. Quoted in GM Corporate Newsroom, "Cadillac's Electric Self Starter Turns 100," February 15, 2012. http://media.gm.com.
39. Quoted in Jessica Easto, ed., *Rocket Man: Elon Musk in His Own Words*. Chicago: Agate, 2017, p. 61.
40. Quoted in Easto, *Rocket Man*, p. 62.
41. Ben Stewart, "2016 Toyota Prius First Drive," *Autoweek*, November 18, 2015. www.autoweek.com.
42. Chuck Squatriglia, "Every New Car Will Be a Hybrid by 2020," *Wired*, August 14, 2008. www.wired.com.
43. US Environmental Protection Agency, "EPA and NHTSA Set Standards to Reduce Greenhouse Gases and Improve Fuel

Economy for Model Years 2017–2025 Cars and Light Trucks," 2012. https://nepis.epa.gov.

44. Nicholas Gerbis, "What Is the Economic Impact of Hybrid Cars?," HowStuffWorks, December 20, 2010. http://auto .howstuffworks.com.

45. Quoted in John O'Dell, "UPS Launching World's First Fuel Cell Electric Class 6 Delivery Truck," Trucks.com, May 2, 2017. www.trucks.com.

46. Quoted in Andrew J. Hawkins, "Electric Cars Are Now Required to Make Noise at Low Speeds So They Don't Sneak Up and Kill Us," The Verge, November 16, 2016. www.theverge .com.

47. Jon Linkov, "Collision-Avoidance Systems Are Changing the Look of Car Safety," *Consumer Reports*, December 17, 2015. www.consumerreports.com.

48. Bob O'Donnell, "Your Average Car Is More Code-Driven than You Think," *USA Today*, June 28, 2016. www.usatoday.com.

49. Alastair Hayfield, "Video: Electronic Technology in the Automotive Industry: What's the Impact?," *Automotive Blog*, IHS Markit, May 20, 2014. http://blog.ihs.com.

50. David L. Strayer et al., *Visual and Cognitive Demands of Using In-Vehicle Infotainment Systems*. Washington, DC: AAA Foundation for Traffic Safety, p. 42.

Chapter 5: A New Automotive Age

51. General Motors, "The Story of Firebird II 'Three-Zero-Two.' The Gas Turbine Family Car, General Motors Latest 'Laboratory on Wheels,'" *Motorama*. www.oldcarmanuals.com.

52. Quoted in *San Francisco Chronicle*, "Autonomous Car Completes Cross-Country U.S. Trip," April 2, 2105. www.sfgate .com.

53. Chris Urmson, Video, Waymo. www.waymo.com.

54. Steve Mahan, Video, Waymo. www.waymo.com.

55. Andy Greenberg, "Hackers Remotely Kill a Jeep on the Highway—with Me in It," *Wired*, July 21, 2015. www.wired .com.

56. Greenberg, "Hackers Remotely Kill a Jeep on the Highway—with Me in It."

57. Greenberg, "Hackers Remotely Kill a Jeep on the Highway—with Me in It."

58. Quoted in Ed Markey, United States Senator for Massachusetts, "Senator Markey and Blumenthal Reintroduce Legislation to Improve Cybersecurity of Vehicles and Airplanes," March 22, 2017. www.markey.senate.gov.

59. Quoted in Andy Patrizio, "Pros and Cons of Artificial Intelligence," Datamation, July 7, 2016. www.datamation.com.

60. Jeremy Hsu, "When It Comes to Safety, Autonomous Cars Are Still 'Teen Drivers,'" *Scientific American*, January 18, 2017. www.scientificamerican.com.

61. Quoted in Lauren Keating, "The Driverless Car Debate: How Safe Are Autonomous Vehicles?," *Tech Times*, July 28, 2015. www.techtimes.com.

62. Eric Tingwall, "How Would Level 5 Cars Change Our Lives?," *Car and Driver*, November 2017, p. 84.

63. James Arbib and Tony Seba, "Rethinking Transportation 2020–2030: The Disruption of Transportation and the Collapse of the Internal-Combustion Vehicle and Oil Industries," RethinkX, May 2017. www.rethinkx.com.

64. Tingwall, "How Would Level 5 Cars Change Our Lives?"

65. Quoted in Chester Dawson, "Your Next Car May Be a Living Room on Wheels," *Wall Street Journal*, June 19, 2017. www.wsj.com.

66. Ale Resnik, "Uber Won't Kill Car Ownership," *Fortune*, August 24, 2016. www.fortune.com.

67. Quoted in Ericsson, "Self-Driving Future: Consumer Views on Letting Go of the Wheel and What's Next for Autonomous Cars," 2017. www.ericsson.com.

GLOSSARY

artificial intelligence (AI): The ability to simulate human thought and behavior by a machine, especially a computer.

autonomous vehicle: A vehicle that operates independently, without human input.

biofuel: A fuel that comes from once-living matter.

chassis: The frame of a car or truck.

concept car: A prototype vehicle that showcases new technology or design.

embargo: A ban on trade with a foreign country.

gas guzzler: A car that consumes large quantities of fuel.

greenhouse gas: A by-product of gasoline exhaust that lingers in the atmosphere and causes temperatures to rise, similar to a florist's greenhouse.

hybrid: An automobile that uses both gasoline and electric power, either separately or together.

magneto: A device that generates electricity magnetically to create a spark in an internal combustion engine.

muscle car: A high-performance automobile with a powerful engine, popular in the 1960s and 1970s.

planned obsolescence: Changing a car's design or features annually to entice customers to purchase a new vehicle.

smog: A dense, fog-like type of pollution caused by sunlight acting on internal combustion vehicle exhaust.

sustainable: Pertaining to an energy source that is not depleted and can be renewed.

Books

John J. Fialka, *Car Wars: The Rise, the Fall, and the Resurgence of the Electric Car*. New York: Thomas Dunne, 2015.

Lawrence Goldstone, *Drive! Henry Ford, George Selden, and the Race to Invent the Auto Age*. New York: Ballantine, 2016.

Meg Jacobs, *Panic at the Pump: The Energy Crisis and the Transformation of American Politics in the 1970s*. New York: Hill and Wang, 2016.

Sue Macy, *Motor Girls: How Women Took the Wheel and Drove Boldly into the Twentieth Century*. Washington, DC: National Geographic, 2017.

Margo T. Oge, *Driving the Future: Combating Climate Change with Cleaner, Smarter Cars*. New York: Arcade, 2015.

Samuel I. Schwartz, *Street Smart: The Rise of Cities and the Fall of Cars*. New York: PublicAffairs, 2015.

Richard Snow, *I Invented the Modern Age: The Rise of Henry Ford*. New York: Scribner, 2013.

Ashlee Vance, *Elon Musk: Tesla, SpaceX, and the Quest for a Fantastic Future*. New York: Ecco, 2017.

Internet Sources

Alex Davies, "This Is Big: A Robo-Car Just Drove Across the Country," *Wired*, April 3, 2015. www.wired.com.

Paul Goodman, "Advantages and Disadvantages of Driverless Cars," AxleAddict, November 22, 2016. https://axleaddict.com.

N.R. Kleinfeld, "American Way of Life Altered by Fuel Crisis," *New York Times*, September 26, 1983. www.nytimes.com.

Charles Krome, "Henry Ford, the Model T, and the Birth of the Middle Class," *In the Community* (blog), Ancestry, August 10, 2016. https://blogs.ancestry.com.

National Historic Route 66 Federation, "The History of Route 66," 2017. www.national66.org.

Cherise Threewitt, "Do Our Driving Skills Diminish When Technology Takes Over?," HowStuffWorks, October 11, 2017. https://auto.howstuffworks.com.

Websites

Henry Ford (www.thehenryford.org). This website showcases Henry Ford and his inventions, provides information on the Greenfield Village outdoor museum, and has links to a variety of educational information.

History of Cars, Explain That Stuff (www.explainthatstuff.com/historyofcars.html). A highly readable history of the automobile from before the first cars to self-driving vehicles. Includes links to other automotive topics and car museums, plus a bibliography.

How Car Engines Work, HowStuffWorks (https://auto.howstuffworks.com/engine). This website presents a thorough explanation, including diagrams and animation, of how the various types of internal combustion engines work. Includes links to articles on other types of engines.

Hybrid Cars (www.hybridcars.com). This website has complete information on hybrid vehicles from the world's automobile manufacturers. It includes facts on different types of hybrid technology, explains how hybrids impact society, and compares fuel efficiency of the various hybrid models.

Motor Vehicle Safety: Impaired Driving, Centers for Disease Control and Prevention (www.cdc.gov/motorvehiclesafety/impaired_driving/index.html). This website presents comprehensive information about the dangers of driving while impaired. Includes statistics and laws for each state and links to important topics such as teen drinking and driving.

INDEX